Climbing the Fish's Tail

The Fish's Tail from the North East : Rock Gendarme on right, Rock Buttress in cloud; upper part of route lay near right-hand sky-line

Climbing the Fish's Tail

by
Wilfrid Noyce

BOOK FAITH INDIA
Delhi

Climbing the Fish's Tail

Published by
BOOK FAITH INDIA
414-416 Express Tower, Azadpur Commercial Complex
Delhi, India 110 033

Distributed by
PILGRIMS BOOK HOUSE
P.O. Box 3872, Kathmandu, Nepal
P.O. Box 38, Varanasi, India
Fax 977-1-424943.
E-mail: info@pilgrims.wlink.com.np
Website: http://www.gfas.com/pilgrims

Cover Design by Pilgrims Publication

ISBN 81-7303-100-2

Printed in India

Contents

CONTENTS

APPENDICES

vi

Illustrations

PLATES

FOR
JEREMY

Preface

THIS IS THE RECORD of a mountain expedition to
Nepal in the spring of 1957. The mountain is Machapuchare (Nepali for "The Fish's Tail"). It is also a
tribute to the beauty of that mountain, the most beautiful
that I, or I think any of us, have climbed. It is natural
to wish to record such beauty, setting the mountain, on
its superlative pedestal, among the deep valleys of Nepal
sprinkled with villages of kindly Gurung men and women.
As one looked at it in the early light from a sleeping-bag
at Chomrong, it was not difficult to agree that Machapuchare must be sacred, that a goddess must dwell upon
that cloven summit; in short, to share the superstition of
the Gurungs and to want to appreciate their attitude to
other things. To them too this book is dedicated.

The reason why it is written by me is that I was
thought (correctly) by the others to have a weakness for
the pen. But it belongs properly to James Roberts, the
leader who first conceived and then collected the
expedition, and whose bold inspiration it was, in 1956,
to tackle that long north ridge. Circumstances unkindly

snatched from him the part that was his due. The book belongs also to Roger Chorley, David Cox and Charles Wylie, who have had their share in making it and whose pictures help to illustrate it. In fact, we are all responsible.

Like all expeditions, we owe a debt to many people, and those who helped us with food and equipment are thanked separately at the end of the book. We would thank first the Government of Nepal for giving us permission to go, and Field-Marshal Kaiser for his good will and hospitality. We would thank Field-Marshal Sir Gerald Templer, C.I.G.S. and Air Chief Marshal Sir Dermot Boyle for their personal interest and practical assistance; also the Air Ministry, Transport Command and Movement Staff; the Everest Foundation for a generous grant; T. Stevenson and the Royal Geographical Society for advice on map making and the loan of a survey instrument; the British Ambassador at Kathmandu for help and encouragement throughout, and with his name and that of Mrs. Tollinton we would join those of Colonel and Mrs. Proud, and the Embassy Staff. Also we would thank the Officers and Staff at the Gurkha Depot, Lehra, for great help and hospitality, and the *Statesman* of Calcutta for its contribution to our funds. For help on our journey through India we are indebted to H.Q. British Gurkhas in India, Miss Mary Cosh and the U.K. High Commission, New Delhi, I.C.I. Pakistan and India, Burma Shell, R. Hotz of New Delhi, and many more who gave us or our luggage a push along the way.

A special word of thanks needs to be said to the British

Women's Hospital at Pokhara, for all that they did when Roger Chorley contracted poliomyelitis. It would be impossible to overestimate our debt to their energy, their nursing skill and their advice, or the difference that these made to his recovery. With mention of them should be joined that of the men of Chomrong who carried him down, Maurice Wilson who accompanied him in the plane home and all others who facilitated his passage.

In preparing the book I have to thank C. Douglas Milner for untiring work, despite other commitments, with the photographs; J. Allen Cash and D. N. Paton for reproductions; G. S. Holland of the Royal Geographical Society and Richard Taylor for maps; Charles Evans for his very fine colour photograph; and last but not least, A. C. Pigou for reading the text and for constructive comments and Mrs. M. H. Ryder for proofreading.

Godalming, 1958   WILFRID NOYCE

Climbing
the Fish's Tail

CHAPTER ONE

Background and Reconnaissance

BY JAMES ROBERTS

FROM THE COUNTRY thirty or forty miles north of the town of Gorakhpur in the province of Uttar Pradesh in Northern India there is a view which has become part of my life. From there on a winter day, provided there is not too much dust haze, or better perhaps on one of those silver and blue days of the dying monsoon, the remote snows contrasting with the furnace of a hot season not yet spent, you can see to the north the high snow mountains of the Central Nepal Himalaya.

The foreground is flat plain, stretching away in a patch-work of rice fields, sugar cane, dal and wheat and dotted with groves of dusty-green mango trees. Beyond and two or three thousand feet above the plain are the green and blue wooded foothills, and seventy miles farther and twenty-three thousand feet higher are the mountains.

The hundred-mile-long white wave we are looking at stretches from Putha Hiunchuli east to Himalchuli: Putha is 23,750 feet high and Himalchuli is 25,801 feet.

Between are higher mountains, and some of the great names of the Himalaya. Annapurna, the 'first of 8,000 metres', the scene of the great French effort of 1950, Dhaulagiri, last of the giants and still inviolate at the end of 1957, and Manaslu, so long besieged by the Japanese. And appearing as part of the crest of the wave, but in fact jutting eight miles south of it, is Machapuchare, the twin-topped 'Fish's Tail' Mountain of Central Nepal, in appearance and character, as well as in local legend, belief and song, dominating its higher rivals to the north.

Between these mountains are the deep river valleys, Kali, Modi, Seti, Marsyandi and Buri Gandaki, which fascinate almost as much as the mountains, flowing as they do out of the mountains and down past the villages of the people that make this country so much more than an inanimate huddle of hills.

These people are as diverse as the country they live in; they range from the pure Indian of the southern Terai, the cultivated flat lands which merge into the sal forest lapping the foothills, to the pure Tibetan of the northern valleys. But the proud princes of this land are the Mongolian hill tribes who live on the southern flanks of the main Himalayan range, and along the long ridges and tangle of green and brown dappled hills which crowd southwards from the snows and eventually overlook the Gangetic plain.

These tribes, in Central Nepal, are the Puns, Magars and Gurungs, and collectively known to us as Gurkhas they have fought and served under British officers in the

4

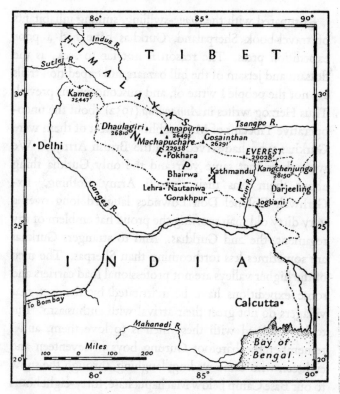

British and Indian armies for nearly one hundred and fifty years. Their precise origin is obscure. Many years ago their forefathers spilt over the lip of the barren uplands of what is now Tibet into the fat valleys of the south. But in character and physiognomy they differ from Tibetans, and it is probable that these wanderers from the north overlaid and swallowed up some earlier population.

Compared with the *chang*-swilling, smiling inhabitants of travel-book Sherpaland, Gurkhas have had a poor expedition press. The reason is not far to seek, as the flotsam and jetsam of the hill bazaars and expedition trails are not the people I write of, and misconceptions prevail. Thus Herzog writes in *Annapurna* (1952) about the uncooperative Tibetans of Manangbhot: "Most of them were Gurkhas who had served with the British Army." We were there that same year and the only Gurkha thing about them was their cast-off Army clothing. Ex-Garhwali Colonel Don Lowndes laughed long over a very dirty old man sporting the proud hat emblem of my regiment, the 2nd Gurkhas. And to strangers Gurkhas are sometimes less forthcoming than Sherpas. The men of the higher valleys are not professional load carriers and some expeditions have been irritated by the fact that villagers do not greet their arrival with enthusiasm. But to have served with these men is to love them, and I remember the barefoot Gurung boys of seventeen and eighteen who came wading, laughing, through the snow to our Base Camp below Machapuchare, forty-eight hours after they had received our SOS that Roger had to be carried down.

Such are the mountains, the rivers and the people of the country that we have been looking at. What is difficult to realise is how recently this country has become known to the outside world. In 1936 Charles Bruce, Gurkha officer and doyen of Himalayan explorers of his day, could write (and his words were still true at least ten

6

years later), ". . . . the great massif of Dhaulagiri, Machapuchare and Annapurna . . . at least four of them exceed 27,000 feet (*sic*). . . . There is, too, almost underlying this great centre, a town and a great mart which has always attracted my curiosity almost beyond any other town in Nepal. No one has been there, no one has seen it, but we know that its climate is almost tropical, that it cannot be more than 2,500 feet in altitude, that it is on the banks of a great lake and that it is in an open valley and lies almost immediately at the foot of these magnificent giants. Phewa Tal is the name of the lake and Pokhara the name of the town."

Heady stuff, this, for a boy who had already climbed for several years at home and in the Alps, and who joined a Gurkha Battalion in India in 1937. To see Pokhara and Machapuchare and the villages in which my men lived, and especially the Gurungs, soon became an obsession. But in those days the interior of Nepal was a forbidden land, more securely closed than ever Mecca or Lhasa in their hey-day. And although the passing years brought other Himalayan explorations, Nepal had to wait. In 1949 a crack appeared in the expedition door, and in 1950 it opened far enough for me to slip in.

It was that year that we saw Machapuchare from close quarters for the first time. Coming from the north we had toiled up onto a 22,000-foot shoulder of Annapurna II, and on to the crest of the main Himalayan range. To the south and at the level of about 20,000 feet lay a thick blanket of monsoon cloud, stretching into the horizon, and to the south-west, rising rudely out of the cloud, were two enormous pillars of ice, leaning and fused together, shining with wet precipice and scabby with cornice and ice-fall. Machapuchare was a challenge which found then no answer, at any rate in my heart. I was tired, I was hungry and I was cold, and my feet were freezing. Later I would remember the vision, but for the moment I was strictly occupied with the present.

That autumn I walked across with the Sherpa Da Namgyal to Pokhara. I was the first Englishman into my private Mecca. The mountains were clouded when we arrived. During the night I was awakened by the moon shining through the thin canvas of the tent, and I dragged my sleeping-bag out into the open. There was Machapuchare shining in the moonlight, a great white pyramid incredibly aloof.

So Machapuchare became for me the ideal of a mountain, a personal possession yet out of this world, unattainable but mine by illogical right, brooding over a country and a people which would shape the rest of my life.

But to me at that time Machapuchare was not meant for climbing, and it took sterner spirits to think of this. In 1953 Basil Goodfellow examined the mountain from the south and from the south-east and drew not un-optimistic conclusions. In 1955, before I left Malaya to take up a Gurkha recruiting appointment in India, Charles Wylie lightly charged me to "have a look" at the mountain. Charles and I had belonged to the same regiment and had climbed a little together in India at the beginning of the war. After the war, apart from a memorable Alpine season in 1947, our paths had diverged, and a climbing partnership which had once seemed natural had never materialised. However in 1957 we were to put this right, and in 1956 I was to find a suitable objective for an expedition the following year. "Encircle the mountain, find a route." He had never seen 'the mountain'. I had. I agreed with grumpy good humour but intended first to scout among the peaks of the Dhaulagiri Himal, twenty-four and twenty-five thousanders, which Ang Nyima and I had looked at from Putha Hiunchuli in 1954.

March 1956 was an unsettling month. Before the Nepal permit came through, John Hartog wrote asking me to join his Mustagh Tower party to the Karakoram. I was sorely tempted, and for a night lived again with the upper Indus running through my sleep. But the next morning Machapuchare and Dhaulagiri were looking at me questioningly through the black rift of a storm which had brought the rustle of rain and almost a smell of the snows down into our plains. So it was Nepal. And then cholera broke out in the foothills and along the walking route to Dhaulagiri, so it was by air to Pokhara and Machapuchare.

On 9th April 1956 we jolted to a halt on Pokhara airstrip. 'We' were my henchman Ang Nyima, a Sherpa who has climbed nearly as high as Tenzing, Lalbahadur Gurung, an athletic child of about seventeen, and myself (forty). The hunt was on but our start was not meteoric. One hot day we lingered in Pokhara collecting porters and then another in Dhumpus, changing most of them. But from Dhumpus I could survey the mountain and make a plan. The Fish's Tail of Machapuchare consists of two summits, 22,958 and 22,935 feet high, about half a mile apart and arranged neatly north and south of each other. From Pokhara only the southern, lower summit is visible, and the mountain presents a symmetrical, sharp-pointed triangular face. The left-hand side of the triangle is the south-west ridge of which Basil Goodfellow had written: "We believe that this ridge could be climbed by a really determined party who were prepared to tackle first-class alpine difficulties at 20,000 to 23,000 feet." This ridge will be climbed one day, but in my opinion will present more than first-class alpine difficulties, as we use the term today. Goodfellow continued: "The south-east ridge has less to commend it. . . . The east flank is not to be thought of. We did not see its western face." This assessment of the east approach was after a very cursory examination only, but certainly from Annapurna it had looked unpromising. So westwards it was for me, and the way lay up the Modi Khola.

As one moves west from Pokhara the northern summit slowly appears, its enormous craggy head leaning perilously out in a vain attempt to look round and over the shoulder of its lower twin on to the roofs of a town it has never seen. My object now was to find out whether it might be possible to gain the gap between the

Machapuchare from the fields of Pokhara

The party : standing, L to R-Roberts, Cox, Dikshya Man (liaison officer). Sittin
L to R-Dhanbahadur, Noyce, Chorley, Wylie, Ang Nyima, Ang Tsering, Tash

Gurkha girl

two summits from the west or, failing that, to try and work round the mountain and examine it from the north.

In one day from Dhumpus we reached Landrung, the highest inhabited village on the east bank of the Modi. Landrung is not much of a place, and is dominated by its opposite number of the west bank, Ghandrung. About 1,500 feet higher and six times the size, the solid, square-housed village metropolis of Ghandrung glowers down in disdain on little Landrung. The villagers said there was no way up the river from their side, and indeed there did not appear to be. With a sigh of relief Landrung pushed us across to Ghandrung.

Ghandrung had looked close, but it took a long time getting there, toiling up 3,000 feet from the Modi. I marched into Ghandrung with some emotion, as in the very early years of my service in a Gurkha battalion I had once discovered that my nickname among the men was 'Ghandrung'. I was never quite certain whether to be gratified or not by this name, which evidently had something to do with my current efforts to learn Gurungkura, Ghandrung being *par excellence* a place of the Gurungs. So here I was at last, entering into my own kingdom. However on this first visit Ghandrung put out no flags, no red carpets. The elders were not overjoyed to hear of my proposed movements: there was no food, near famine prevailed (the smiling boys looked sleek and well nourished): it was just possible there might be a path up the Modi gorge (grudgingly, this), but from what I could make out the route sounded suitable only for a gymnastic baboon. However there was a higher village, Chomrong, and Chomrong would have to decide our fate. With a sigh of relief Ghandrung pushed us up to Chomrong.

Chomrong (well-beloved Chomrong of green, well-watered lawns, golden barley and painted houses at the very foot of Ganesh and Machapuchare) was more matey. We asked for a sheep, a guide and permission to proceed. One by one the people wandered away and we were left by ourselves.

After a time some of the village elders returned, and a little old hunchback was their spokesman. Yes, there was a path up the gorge, but no outsider had ever been up. A couple of years before, some surveyors had set up a camp and a 'flag' on that hill over there, and they tried to look into the gorge and up to its head. They stayed there for a fortnight of mist and rain and never a glimpse did the Goddess give the beggars of Her Sanctuary. For a powerful Goddess lived at the top of the gorge and Machapuchare, Ganesh and Hiunchuli were Her dwelling-places.

Yes, we could go, but we must abide by certain rules. The first stage was Kuldighar, and the second the great cave of Hinko. Between the two were the grazing ground of Tomon, and a little farther on the shrine of Panchenin Barha, at the very neck of the gorge. Beyond Tomon no person of a menial caste could proceed, and beyond the shrine we must not take the flesh of chicken or cow or pig. The Goddess must be propitiated at the shrine and suitable places beyond by the offering of small gifts and *dhaja*, streamers of coloured cloth. And that expensive sheep they were about to sell us might well make an appropriate sacrifice.

The dietary restrictions imposed by the Goddess caused at first sight few hardships. A small bottle of Bovril decorated with a bull's head obviously came under the ban, but a tin of sausages I passed on the grounds that it seemed unlikely that even the manufacturers knew what they were made of. But one day out, at Kuldi, came the great egg bombshell. A small but welcome gift of eggs was accompanied by the soul-chilling words: "Cook 'em for the Sahib's breakfast, no eggs allowed beyond Tomon." After that I kept off the subject of food and drink.

At Tomon we paused to drop off a Kami porter, divide up his load and to cache our stock of fifty eggs. Ang Nyima, possibly apprehensive of the testy temper of a Sahib faced with an eggless month, was openly scornful, but I insisted on keeping to the rules. We passed Panchenin Barha and left our *dhaja*, a few annas and some cigarettes as a peace offering. In a cold drizzle of rain we reached the Hinko cave. The porters now left us. Monal pheasant whistled in the mists and I disturbed a thar, a Himalayan wild goat, at a range of a few yards. The way through the gorge had not been difficult, but unpleasant for long stretches with wet slabs and slippery, bamboo-floored thickets. The Hinko cave, at about 9,500 feet, was more romantic than comfortable, the vortex of many winds and draughts. But we made it our base for the first few days, while we explored up the valley and relayed loads.

In mountaineering there are few thrills more exhilarating than the excitement of penetrating new country, of turning a rock buttress and seeing round the corner a route, or no route at all, up some desired mountain. And if one can call 'new' a country which had already been penetrated right up to the summer snow-line by Gurung shepherds, the days that followed were full of this thrill.

With growing excitement I began to realise that there might be a route up our mountain. Direct assault from the west was out of the question, but the higher summit gave off a long ridge to the north, sinking one and a half miles from the summit to a col at about 19,500 feet. If the crest of this ridge was passable it seemed that there might be a continuation on to the north summit. It became our object to gain a viewpoint from which the crest of the ridge could be seen end-on, instead of in profile, and its width and difficulty assessed.

We failed in this object, but from our farthest point could see that the upper portion of the ridge seemed to merge into a snow-field and that this snow-field should provide a base and camp site from which the very steep, but not vertical, final 1,000-foot ice-cliff defending the north summit could be tackled. We also failed to get across the Modi river, and thus to prove the very lowest portion of the route to the north col, a 1,000-foot rock curtain above the river. The way lay up a deep sinister rift in the rock, Gardyloo Gully, whose twists and turns

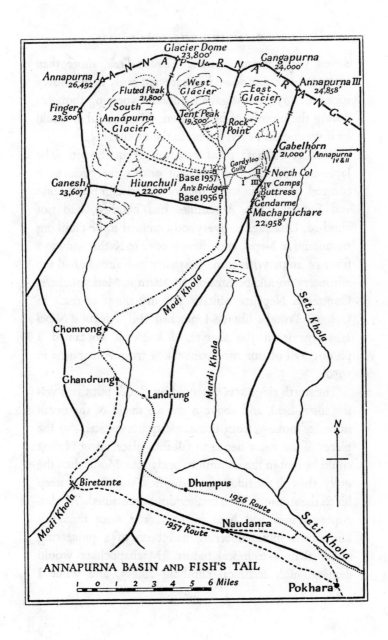

ANNAPURNA BASIN AND FISH'S TAIL

1 0 1 2 3 4 5 6 Miles

defied visual reconnaissance. *Gardez l'eau*, more than water might come down here: it went easily in the snowy spring of 1957, but it gave me many worrying thoughts during the months of preparation. How awful it would be if we couldn't even get on to the mountain!

Back in Pokhara great events were in the air. The Japanese had climbed Manaslu and were even now camped on the air strip: the Swiss had climbed Lhotse and Everest. The Argentines had climbed, had not climbed, Dhaulagiri. Everybody seemed to be climbing mountains in Nepal, and I flew at once to Kathmandu in a fever of anxiety lest some trespasser had already had the effrontery to ask permission to attempt Machapuchare. Courteous Nepalese officials put my mind at rest. In Colonel Proud's library I plucked Bill Tilman's *Nepal Himalaya* from the shelves. I knew it contained a photograph of our mountain taken from Annapurna in 1950.

The north ridge was obscured by cloud, but there was the snow-field, and above it the ice shield of the north summit, looking from this angle quite vertical. So the pieces of the route began to fall into place. Ang Nyima could be sent in the autumn to bridge the Modi; then the gully, the col, the ridge, the snow-field and the very steep bit to the summit. One further doubt remained. My last Alpine season had been in 1947, and since then my Himalayan mountaineering had been of a pioneering rather than a technical nature. Machapuchare would demand high technical climbing ability, and while I might organise and show the way, on the mountain someone else would have to take over.

In broad outline, though not in precise detail, the climb went as it had been planned. And in Wilfrid Noyce we found our mountain leader.

CHAPTER TWO

The Modern Lodestone

What, after all, are formations like these?
Stratified rocks, if you come to consider,
Placed at an angle of x-ty degrees.
                    —A. D. GODLEY

SHAKESPEARE, or rather his Benedick, thought it strange that a sheep's guts should have power to hale souls out of men's bodies. The substance of a mountain, usually crumbly rock held together by glue-like ice and powdered with snow-dust, is as commonplace, and yet has as strange properties, as the guts of any sheep. Mountaineers therefore do well to ask the same question: why there are some shapes that make them dream at night and day-dream in their waking hours. Why the scientifically explicable should be spiritually inexplicable but neverthe-less compelling. Why they have to go.

With some mountains, like Everest with its supremacy in height and its tradition, there is a plausible excuse for accepting a job to be done and getting on with it. Others are almost incidental to journeys which are adding 'Useful

SUMMIT

ROCK
GENDARME

ROCK
BUTTRESS

THE NICK

CAMP III

SNOW
HUMP

NORTH
COL

SECOND
CAMP II

FIRST
CAMP II

Machapuchare from the west

Tashi, Ang Tsering and Ang Nyima receive clothing from Roberts

Machapuchare from above Naudanra

Knowledge' to the world's geographical store. Or again, there are the hills near home, the climbing of which is, among other things, a relaxation from the unease of civilised life. But the smaller Himalayan climbing expedition has no such justifications. It is not purposeful and big like an Everest venture, justifying itself nationally and even having funds provided for it. Nor does it usually contribute much geographical information; while as for holidays, three or four months at a stretch are more than the most cavalier member of the Welfare State could reasonably allow himself on that pretext.

No, the urge to climb remains a kink or flaw in the otherwise reasonable personality. It cannot be explained, except in terms of those soul-haling shapes. After Everest, splendid as a corporate venture but illuminated in retrospect by "a light that never was, on sea or land", it had already seemed to me that the picture would be complete if I could go back to the magnetic Himalaya on a smaller scale, as I had gone before in Garhwal and Sikkim and Kashmir. The natural sequel to that was the postcard which arrived in midsummer of 1956 from Charles Wylie: "Jimmy Roberts says, what about trying Machapuchare next year? Only seven days from an airfield. . . . Can you give me David Cox's address?"

I could, and did. David and I had climbed together often in the Alps; but it needed this stimulus to goad our respectably married selves into calling—albeit with an uneasy conscience—once more upon the generosity of our nearest and dearest. It has always been an astonishment to me that the Victorians, and even the men of Scott's generation, should have departed for such long periods with so little apparent concern. Times change, and we are grateful for that fact in that it shortens our absence. But the human heart and its fears cannot change. Besides, in our case there were nine children to be left and looked after, when you count Charles's four.

The first 'meeting' therefore, at the restaurant of *La Belle Étoile* in Soho, took place in the convivially grateful mood of schoolboys who have been allowed off on some unexpectedly unforbidden jaunt. Indeed our truancy was emphasised, quite apart from our families, by our jobs. David, a don, had succeeded in persuading Oxford that nobody really learns any history in the summer term anyway; Charterhouse had given me its blessing maybe on the understanding that much the same was true of Modern Languages. Charles would be taking this as part of his leave, on the way back to join his Gurkha battalion in Malaya. For Jimmy too it would be leave, though heaven knew how he had managed it, after the reconnaissance of 1956. He is a strong-minded person, and he had fallen badly in love with the mountain.

Charles brought out photographs, and the fascination of the mountain's superb lines had their chance to play on us to the full. Each has his own taste, and the sight of a small boat on dark waters does not stir me greatly. But this hugely poised mass of rock, vertical-sided (as it looks from the south) and cloven at the top into the twin summits that give it 'the Fish's Tail' for name—this moved me unaccountably. I started to dream already, and missed a good deal of the conversation. At the same time I was well aware how calmly most people would regard that photograph. Suppose I rushed out into the street with it, and thrust it under somebody's nose!

"What do you think of that?"

"Bit of rock, is it? Looks like a fish-tail all right. . . . Only bigger, of course."

But in the restaurant it was warm, and we talked on. I had a specimen high altitude boot from Haynes & Cann, who were good friends of ours throughout and finally produced a splendidly warm and comfortable boot. We looked at this prototype with interest; so did the waiters. Then we allotted ourselves jobs. Jimmy, *primum mobile* and leader of the expedition, was in India already, at the Gurkha Depot of which he was in command. He was arranging permissions, engaging Sherpas, working out quantities and coolie loads, of which he had already sent an impressive list. Charles, who worked at the War Office and had his experience as Secretary of the Everest Expedition, was inevitably secretary again. Most of the work fell on his back; and it was pleasant, turning to him, to have the same feeling of confidence as in 1952. David had the thankless task of treasurer, the more thankless because he would be called upon to juggle with three altering currencies. I got off with the climbing equipment and other oddments.

We agreed that we would need a lot of rope, from the look of Jimmy's north ridge—perhaps 3,000 feet. And pitons, or pegs, to fix it with, and of course karabiners, or snap-rings. We were strangely matter-of-fact about it all, now that I look back, considering that this would probably be a harder peak than any of us had attempted, even in the Alps. I think that our chief determination was to be safe, and then hope for luck. Hence the ropes. If we got up, so much the better. If not, well, we would have had a good 'do', and there were other peaks at hand.

We sat there a long time. One of the waiters, whether in impatience or moved by our enthusiasm, volunteered to join the expedition as cook. We thanked him, but regretfully declined.

*　　*　　*

The little things. It seems strange that there are so many of them, and yet so it is, every time. We were only doing what many have done since the war, and go on doing. The process ought to become progressively easier, since each party learns from the others, and yet each makes most of the same mistakes over again, with variations of its own. It was a busy time, specially for Charles, but with a business so much a matter of routine nowadays that I shall comment on only one or two characteristic features.

Mike Ward had been going to join us; but medical men are too much in demand these days and he could not make it. "Who else?" Charles said, and I answered: "Roger Chorley, if he can come." We breathed a big sigh of relief when he could. But we still had no doctor, and the possibility of Hamish Nichol hung for a short time in the balance. But he had a new post and could not make it either. In the end the duties of medical officer devolved upon me, my claim to that title resting chiefly on a lively hour with Jo Waycott, Charterhouse M.O., over glasses of Dubonnet. I took copious notes in an unsteady hand, and followed them with a request to Mike Ball, who gave generously of his Himalayan experience. Medical stores converged slowly; we were helped by the Mustagh Tower party, as well as by Charterhouse and British Drug Houses.

Preparations for a small party of this sort go so informally that it would be hard to distinguish them exactly from those of a long Alpine season. Charles applied for a grant from the Everest Foundation, and we received a handsome one. He succeeded in getting our kit packed up (by Edgington) and the bulk of it despatched on the P. & O. cargo ship *Chinkoa* at the end of January. Suez was still closed. We would discuss the latest from India over the phone, or in long letters exasperating to our families at the breakfast table. Permission was not so difficult to come by, particularly for Jimmy with his Nepalese connection through the Gurkhas. But it appeared that we would have to pay an entrance fee, how much was not at first known. The Nepalese Government, partly in indignation at the antics of a British party in West Nepal in 1955, had decided to impose new restrictions which included a tariff on all peaks. Everest headed the list at 3,000 rupees (about £225); a tiddler like Machapuchare cost only 1,000. It was while we were in Nepal that the Abominable Snowman beat Everest and had his single life valued at 5,000 rupees. I think the Government has every right to require payment. If you have a country composed largely of unproductive mountains, and none of the facilities of the Swiss, then why not charge those who are foolish enough to come scrambling over their sides and chilling their blood on the tops? Besides, the anomalies in this excellent system will in time be ironed out. There is no rebate, of course, if you do not get up your selected peak; and when Jimmy asked about going up another summit, unnamed and therefore having no tariff price attached, the question caused some slight doubt. It appeared also that we would have to have a liaison officer, to be fed, clothed and paid by us.

David had headaches with the moneys and bought Primus spares in quantity, for he was also in charge of kitchen necessaries. Roger Chorley, an accountant, was active everywhere and in everything. Besides reducing an average age which had been veering perilously close on forty, he modernised our ice standards. In our calculations for pitons and rope, as well as in our methods on the mountain, we owed great debts to the experience of others, particularly John Hartog's Mustagh Tower party which had been faced with a rather similar problem, and which generously shared its findings. In conception, of course, we owed nothing, since Jimmy had had the idea, and planned the reconnaissance, before he heard that the Tower was to be attacked. Roger was in charge of food, and had learnt a lot from his Rakaposhi expedition of 1954, particularly from George Band. I remember the formidable chart which unfurled itself, in Charles's office, over half the table. He also organised our still photography; while Charles induced B.B.C. Television to give 3,000 feet of cine film.

I had not realised to what extent the modern adventurer is compelled to go round, cap in hand, begging the means to go venturing. On Everest we had been royally catered for, and my previous trips had been so small that I could buy or borrow on Indian soil. But now—it was a sobering experience. I was to write articles, and one of my tasks therefore was to batter at the doors of editorial offices in the hope of raising a few pounds by so doing. I sent the photographs, which would be returned with admiring comment. "We agree the pictures are very striking. But . . ." Papers were divided between those which did not go in for mountaineering articles, and those which had had so many that they did not want any more just now. The *Statesman*, of Calcutta, took a series, and I was very thankful. Demoralisation had been setting in. I had not wanted to flog myself around, but when I made the effort, for our overdraft's sake . . . ! I was grateful also to John Johnson, my literary agent, for taking the rebuffs.

We had no desire to commit ourselves to a book. It may be true, in Dr. Johnson's phrase, that "no man but a blockhead ever writes except for money", but shortness of pocket seemed no justification for agreeing in advance to commit what might prove a bad story to paper, and thence to an overcrowded book market. There might be nothing to write about. After all, it was only a small giant, as giants go, and suppose we got up easily? Or failed miserably? Better to wait.

Personal arrangements for a journey have a similar feel about them, whether you are bound for Liverpool or Lhasa. Tickets must be bought, for the first stage which will be shared by dozens of your fellows. The main baggage has gone off, and what is packed now consists of toothbrush, pyjamas and the like, which are much the same wherever you are going to use them. True, inoculations must be submitted to; but needle punctures are now a matter of everyday occurrence, in England as elsewhere. It all seemed very ordinary.

Occasionally, however, I found myself raising an eye to the horizon and thinking: next week or so I shall be in India, and after that beyond the bounds of habitation. I shall be on what one paper has kindly described as "the hardest peak in the Himalaya" (a meaningless but flattering phrase). I rubbed metaphorical eyes and the haze of dream spread over the reality of teaching, writing, washing up, playing hockey or climbing sandstone. Reality? If this was unreal for me, how much more so for my family and non-climbing friends, who could know even less than I what it would be like 'out there'? Macha-puchare is not reassuring in pictures. Avalanches? Yes, they do happen occasionally, but they won't on this peak, partly because it is steep and its ridges are so sharp. But

then one might fall off? Not really, because by driving
pitons into the ice, and fixing ropes, we shall be sure of
sticking to the mountainside, even if we don't get up it.
With handrails the Sherpa porters will be able to come up
easily, in good or bad weather. What about getting ill?
You're not exactly a well-qualified doctor. Unanswerable questions! Oh for magic words and magic sedatives
to allay doubts that are no less real because they are not
always uttered. I was still musing on reality and unreality,
on good and bad, as we drove to London Airport in the
bright sunshine of 1st April. April Fools' Day. It would
serve me right if the whole thing were a hoax, and myself
the dupe of it.

But the airport was there, solid and busy and intimidat-
ing. The good-byes were said. I sat and waited for
David, who would join up here for the flight.

CHAPTER THREE

Frustration

An inability to stay quiet, an irritable desire to act directly, is one of the most conspicuous failings of mankind.

—WALTER BAGEHOT

FOR ME partings are like going back to school. In prospect they are horrible. Once past, a new prospect substitutes itself, with the pleasures of reunion at the end of the vista. I am all eagerness to be getting on. I think (or hope) that this is not callousness, but the human mechanism adjusting itself to circumstance.

Charles had gone out already, to prepare the way. He had also escorted our air baggage from Karachi to Lehra, beyond Gorakhpur in the province of Uttar Pradesh, where was the Gurkha Depot and our jumping-off point. Roger Chorley would join us at Istanbul. David and I, the last, were full of impatience to be with them.

The first stage of the journey was commonplace to the point of tears. We broke down at Düsseldorf, and had to wait twelve hours. It seemed desperately important to be off, as if we were late for some family reunion. And a whole series of connections depended upon the time of our arrival in Karachi. Feverishly we totted up the hours lost by flying west to east; picked up Roger in the middle of the night; arrived late at Karachi and just missed our connection. However, French Air Lines were able to take us on to New Delhi, and on the morning of the 4th we landed at Gorakhpur. Here Charles met us, looking very tropical, his jeeps manned by small and smiling Gurkhas. We drove the forty odd miles to Lehra, through jungle and fields of dal.

Charles had bad news. The sea kit, which should have been safely lodged at Lehra, had not even reached Calcutta. This meant a delay of at least a week: one week of fume and fret, of doing nothing. We arrived at Lehra, and started to do nothing straight away.

Lehra itself is a tiny Indian village, but a few hundred yards away is the Depot. This consists of rows of mud and stone huts which constitute a village of their own, with their own bazaar and spaces where tents can be pitched at the time of 'air trooping', when Gurkhas arrive by air from Malaya on leave, or return from leave in Nepal to be wafted back to the Malayan jungle. There is an efficient hospital. But by far the most imposing building is the Officers' Mess.

It was in the 1830s that Mr. Bridgman, a gentleman from England, bought a strip of jungle from which he carved a 'zemindari' or estate near Lehra. Such was the practice at that time, and besides Bridgmanganj, named after him, there are other ganjes down the line which still bear the name of once reigning families. Sometimes the families are still there, but they can no longer be said to reign. The cool, fan-laden and bearer-haunted halls of Mr. Bridgman's palace were ideally suited to doing nothing, had we been so inclined. The hospitality of Jimmy's brother officers added its inducements. Nevertheless we fretted, and consumed hours on telephone and wireless. At each call to Calcutta, the *Chinkoa's* arrival date seemed more remote.

Jimmy himself was at Pokhara or Kathmandu, mysteriously employed. He was virtually inaccessible even by wireless, with only Ang Nyima for company. The other three Sherpas were here to greet us, and I should here introduce them, since they will crop up so modestly, almost shyly, throughout the story that their key part can easily be forgotten.

It is now virtually impossible to take Sherpas to the Karakoram, because of Pakistan frontier difficulties, and the visitor to Nepal is therefore in an enviably luxurious position. The brown, smiling little men from Sola Khumbu, the Everest country, have proved themselves now on countless expeditions. Their value lies not only in their load-carrying powers and the climbing skill which they have picked up through the years, but in their general ability to oil wheels and make life agreeable. Of these qualities Tashi, who stood before us now, was a fine example: the Sherpa at his best.

He was small, as the Sherpas are, with skin drawn tight

over the high cheek-bones, narrow eyes and rather prominent teeth, usually visible. His stubby hair was faintly grizzled, his body lean, intensely economical of outline. We knew of him already as the Sherpa who, in 1955, on Kangchenjunga, had enabled the top camp to be pitched by omitting to use all his oxygen, so that George Band found some in a cylinder which revivified the party. In his climbing style he reminded me of a Swiss pater-familias I once met on the Tödi: very competent, entirely safe and a great hewer of steps. He always took the lead when a Sherpa party went up, and I always wondered why he had not made a bigger job of being sirdar, or leader of Sherpas. In camp he was a mainstay, and here the luxury came in. Usually first to get the tea going, he stayed last to finish the washing-up. Did a tent need repairing, a rope ladder constructing? Ask Tashi, and even the implements would be to hand—against all probability. He was what every climber (or housewife) wishes to possess: a treasure.

Ang Tsering was a boy of seventeen, shy and good-looking in a boyish way. I should add that he was already married, indeed was Tashi's son-in-law. The Sherpas have a habit of marrying boys of sixteen or seventeen to girls of twenty-five or more, whence comes their other habit, that of allowing the woman to be boss of the home. They are a very happy people and a good advertisement for the system. One could imagine a daughter of Tashi ruling Ang Tsering, who would be too gentle and gentlemanly to resist the custom. He spoke little at first, but much more, with his charming smile, on the mountain, where he was coached by Tashi in the task of looking after sahibs royally. Slim and beautifully built, he was also very religious, and we would be woken in the morning by the sound of tuneful chanting, sometimes accompanied by the untuneful bass of Ang Nyima. The third Sherpa was Da Temba, a small, ugly man with the air of a quiet comedian (as he turned out to be), the only one of the four to hail from Darjeeling. He looked nervous and was not happy, as it proved, on steep places. But he was an excellent cook, and much happier in the kitchen.

We decided to leave these three and on the 8th to fly, by way of Pokhara, to Kathmandu, which we had hoped to visit anyway, after the expedition. The evening before flying, we saw, from the Mess roof, parts of the Annapurna Himal against a cloudy sky. What looked like a needle of black rock stood out to the right: Machapuchare, about a hundred miles away. We looked at it with emotion, but it seemed quite unreal.

Lehra lies some 40 miles from the frontier town of Nautanwa. On what proved the one hazeless morning we were driven in jeeps across miles of dusty fields in which the harvested dal stood. But our eyes were over the banyan tops, fixed on the whole range spread before us in pink and rusted gold. Dhaulagiri showed nobly on the left, then the enormous bulk of Annapurna I, impressive but to my taste shapeless as Monte Rosa in Ruskin's description, "a haycock after a thunder shower". Then Annapurna III, with the Fish's Tail piercing its

white breast, and IV and II away to the right. It all looked
very near, as near as the Oberland seen from Berne, and
gave no idea of the complexity of ridges.

Beyond Nautanwa, where official documents were
signed and a haze of babus satisfied by Charles, is the little
airfield of Bhairwa. This must be one of the sturdiest air
services in the world: after twenty minutes, over the foothills, the plane is bumping down on a yet more uneven
field—for it is no more—at Pokhara. The pilot told us
that the strip would not meet any of the safety regulations; but there it was, and day after day and several times
a day the Dakotas go swooping across, to discharge their
very mixed loads of penniless-looking peasants who must
have a stocking somewhere, and Gurkha N.C.O.s smart
with all the dignity that starched bottle-green uniform
and broad-brimmed hat can give.

At Pokhara, Machapuchare, which had been waving
like a gigantic finger above the brown foothills, came at
last to rest on our horizon. It still towered over us, seeming, above the palms and pipuls, almost to overlook the
airfield as the Matterhorn overlooks Zermatt. As the
crow flies, it was about 15 miles away. Jimmy Roberts
was at Pokhara, smiling confidence from under a very
British-looking pork-pie hat, and Ang Nyima with his
wide grin. He looked smart and orderly in his role as
Jimmy's batman, and pleased to see us. I remembered
saying good-bye, four years before, outside the Embassy
at Kathmandu in the days of post-Everest celebration.
Ang Nyima had been one of the very best Everest

33

Sherpas, distinguishing himself particularly on the Lhotse Face and in carrying the top camp. For these and other reasons Jimmy had taken him to Lehra as personal servant. The four years had developed for him an ugly abscess in the side, which was to worry him, though not to impede him greatly, on the mountain. But the roguish smile and chuckle were still there, and though he had given up smoking (with Anullu he was about the heaviest smoker on Everest) he still liked a drink. Jimmy had included five bottles of rum among the expedition stores, and these we broached on special occasions. Ang Nyima would collect the four tots for the Sherpas; and it was only at the end of the expedition that we discovered that the other three were virtually teetotal.

It was hot here, for Pokhara is only some 3,000 feet above sea-level, and Jimmy's camp site in a neighbouring field received the full sun. Its one overriding advantage was that from it he could charge each incoming plane, in the hope that it contained our luggage. But there was no other. Water was far to fetch, and of doubtful quality. We met Dhanbahadur, our cook, a sturdy and likeable little Tamang who had formerly been a coolie. Then we prepared to go on.

*　　*　　*

Jimmy, who had just come from Kathmandu where he had been making final arrangements, stayed to guard the airstrip. The rest of us, in a golden afternoon that seemed

A coolie, Gangabahadur

Ghandrung

to lighten the whole range from Dhaulagiri almost to Everest, continued our flight to the city of the little yellow god. In half an hour we were there.

In 1953 I had approached on foot, walking with Mike Westmacott over the hills in the wake of our luggage. Then we had returned amid the jubilations of half a million. This time, with no luggage even in the offing, we seemed to come upon the town with startling suddenness. It was all as it had been, the bumpy roads, the high palace walls, the housefront woodwork of the Newars. Only, this time, there were no thousands in from all over the valley to cheer Tenzing; no triumphal arches, no banners. We had the place to ourselves. Lodged comfortably at the Snow View, one of Kathmandu's rare hotels, we could look around.

We were conscientious sightseers, but those four days remain in memory clouded with a fretful doubt which added to the unreality of the quick air passage and sudden vision of our mountain. Colonel and Mrs. Proud welcomed us hospitably, but were not reassuring. Cargo boats advancing up the east coast of India might take *any* time, might call at *any* port that took their fancy. And even when they arrived at the Hooghly, they were still far from berthed. At the Embassy, where the Ambassador and Mrs. Tollinton entertained us most kindly, we heard that the Yorkshire Ramblers party had had to go down to Calcutta for their luggage. . . . And the weather was getting hotter every day.

We finally rejected Calcutta, after deliberation. We

made the decision, as all others, very much in the manner of a party of friends climbing in the Alps, not of an expedition. Then we turned to sightseeing. In the town itself there is little apart from the crowded streets near Hanuman Doka. I can still see Roger's spare figure, swathed in two cameras, wandering past the ten-foot high god Kali, towards the corner that was the scene of Jung Bahadur's *coup* in 1866, "when the court ran with blood". And I can see the tiny children there, in Technicolor sunlight, chewing betel or sugar cane as they drove their calves past the gods; girls, their round faces a relief after parched India, their bright smooth hair fragrant with sweet peas, their sari-type skirts and white shawls; old men in carpenter hats and tight trousers; wild sadhus or holy men, their faces streaked with white. Through all this the great Brahmini bulls wandered ponderously, pausing to flick a tail or cast a melancholy eye at the hags who crouched over heaps of fly-ridden sweetmeats.

Here Hindu and Buddhist meet, to the foreigner inexplicably. We visited the great Buddhist shrine of Bhodnath, still gay with the myriad prayer-flags of the anniversary celebrations. The Chini Lama introduced a Western note, with his golf jacket and trousers and ideas of buying Colonel Proud's Land-Rover. Swayambunath is an older (and dirtier) Buddhist temple, magnificently sited on a hill-top. But to set against these there are the great Hindu shrines at Patan and Bhadgaon, and a charming temple with wonderful stone carving at Changunarayan, two miles from Bhadgaon over the hot cornfields. Most sacred of all to the Hindus, the stream at Pasupatinath, into which are thrown the ashes of the dead. The temple itself we infidels were not allowed to enter. The fact here seems to be that Buddhism and Hinduism have adopted the wise principle of Asoka, that religions should honour in each other all that is worthy of honour, and so live happily side by side. In the Hindu pantheon Gautama Buddha appears sometimes as a reincarnation of Krishna, while the Buddhist of Kathmandu can see Krishna in lotus posture at the side of Gautama himself.

Our sightseeing was punctuated by desperate rushes to the Embassy, in the hope of a telegram from Lehra about the kit. We began to style ourselves "the expedition that never got started"; and on the 12th, demoralised but determined at any rate to suffer, we boarded the plane once more for Pokhara.

Three important contacts had been made. The first was with Field-Marshal Kaiser, an old friend of Charles's family and a most kind host. The second was with John Nicholls Booth, an American Unitarian Minister who was filming, and who proposed to accompany us on the first stage of the march. Unitarianism in America must be a liberal employer, we thought, for he seemed to have filmed in most parts of the world, taking about a year off in every three. He was a striking but friendly figure, bearded and unruffled. Like many Americans, he had a knack of looking improbable but achieving his object more effectively than we.

Last but not least, we met our liaison officer, Dikshya

Man. The liaison officer can be a valuable institution (as in Pakistan), but we had not expected a youth of twenty, still at college, who had never been out of the Valley. Thick-set, with broad face and thick lips, he showed an admirable enthusiasm for speaking English, but one which made it very difficult for our two fluent Nepali speakers to converse with him, since his English was clearly far less than their Nepali. He came round to greet us in Nepali dress, and we tried to persuade him, in English, that gym shoes were better wear for the march than thin leather. He appeared with a pair on the last day.

The days that followed the 12th are remembered through a haze of lethargy and disappointment. In the morning our peaks showed misty and majestic under the early sun. We lay and looked hungrily. Then the haze set in (we did not know that it was bad weather, up there) and with it hot despondency. Our diet was not varied, as all jams and other tins came with the kit. But we were contracting mild dysentery one by one, so had little appetite anyway.

There were alleviations. Pokhara village lay some two miles away, a big, sprawling, characteristic brick and plaster affair with a hot bazaar up and down which we wandered, trying to get a good exchange from Indian to Nepali rupees. General Bruce might have been disappointed. But just this side of it lived the Hedegards, an American with his family who had the job of teaching modern agriculture to the men of Pokhara. Their kindness and cold drinks were supplemented by the hospitality of the British Women's Hospital Mission, just beyond the village if we had the energy to get there. The three or four Nissen-like buildings of bright metal which form the hospital stood on a green shelf over the Seti Khola (River) and commanded a view of Machapuchare at its most un-believable. On the afternoon of our visit, however, a storm poured itself over the thatched huts in which these isolated and brave women live. I could not help thinking of *Punch's* idea of the Britisher, as the rain whipped in through the windows and occasionally the roof, while tea was passed and fruit cake served as sedately as in any London drawing-room.

The missioners are Christian (there is one man now, Dr. Turner), but their work is medical, not missionary. Miss Steel, who was in charge, told us how they had waited years at the frontier before being allowed in, to spread medicine in regions where it is virtually unknown. They spoke of their hopes of a leper hospital, and of Macha-puchare, 'our mountain'. They could not help hoping that we would not get quite to the top.

Another alleviation was the lake. About a mile to our south-west, green and cool, the Phewa Tal stretched into the distance under wooded hills that might have been those round Buttermere, if you half-shut your eyes. On the northern shore a residence was going up for the King, beautifully sited. Near it we used to bathe, swimming right across to the far shore in an ecstasy that almost made the heat of the day worth bearing. We visualised a future pleasure spot, in the endurable months of the year:

39

"Annapurnaview or Royal Hotel, bathing, boating, fishing, tennis. Excursions to Machapuchare." But the days of tariffs will have to go, and those of Swiss hoteliers to come, before the Nepalese Government realises that dream.

I have said that we were excellently placed for the air-field. On the 16th our routine charge of the incoming plane, instead of sending us once more disappointed back to our tents, revealed at last a message from the Lehra Depot. Captain Tim Bellers would be sending off the kit, which had arrived from Bhairwa, and tomorrow. Tomorrow there it was, to be grasped, hammered open, unpacked by eager Sherpas (for the other arrived with it) and distributed by no less eager sahibs. We were like children, unable to believe that Christmas has really come. Booth, a martyr to his art, filmed our attitudes. Dikshya Man watched. It was a stifling but exciting afternoon.

Word was now given for the fifty coolies arranged by Jimmy to make their appearance and receive advance of pay. As each came up to the packing-case desk his thumb print was taken, a pure formality since we had hardly the C.I.D. equipment to track down defaulters. Still, it impresses the recipients of pay with the importance of their responsibilities. I studied the ragged file, some large, some small, most with Nepali rather than round Gurung faces, all underfed and scantily clothed. There was Ganga-bahadur, a tall, picturesque type with long hair and ear-rings; 'Knobbly-Knees', a little man with enormous calves that would have done credit to a Michael Angelo athlete, recognisable half a mile away; and many more. They all seemed happy.

In the evening we surveyed the untidy jumble of sacks and boxes (the crates had been sold) and wondered if anybody would be able to pick them up. But in the morning the smiling army was back once more, talkatively performing miracles with bits of string. Enormous loads were slung up on to headbands, giving those frail bodies the look of Dante's proud sinners in Purgatory. On the morning of the 18th the expedition straggled off on what is still euphemistically known as a 'march', towards the snows. A bullock team started to plough up our field.

It was coincidence, but a pleasant one, that the street of Pokhara was gay with flowers and red paper decorations. The village was to be visited that day by the King in person.

CHAPTER FOUR

To the Sanctuary and Above It

*They came at a delicate plain, called Ease, where
they went with much content; but that plain was but
narrow, so they went quickly over it. . . . They came
to the Delectable Mountains.*

—BUNYAN

ONLY SEVEN DAYS from Pokhara to Base Camp, this
must be one of the shortest of all Himalayan marches.
When we were on the mountain, it came as a constant
surprise to reflect that the airfield lay only a few miles
away. And once the reflection was to be a source of great
comfort.

The start of the path along the Seti Khola is hot and
dusty. But I shall not forget the first evening, after we
had climbed away from it to Naudanra among the
terraced fields, over 5,000 feet up. We seemed to be
breathing something so unlike the treacly stuff at Pokhara
that the term 'air' could hardly cover both. Walking on
next day to the watershed from which we would drop

Man of Chomrong

Machapuchare from the south-west

westward to the Modi Khola, we passed a Nepali, apparently carrying his lunch in a cloth, while his wife followed in a back-basket behind. It turned out that he had heard of the Pokhara hospital and had been taking her there to have a baby born. But he had miscalculated by a day, and was now on his way back from Naudanra, quite happily, with the baby in his handkerchief.

The terraced fields of rice and maize lost themselves in the besetting haze of that April. At Biretante (3,000 feet), to which we dropped, we left the westerly trade route to Tibet and turned north, along the Modi Khola which we would be following all the way now. Booth left us here, beyond our cool bathe-cum-camp site, and we ceased trying to look like film stars. The parting was cordial, he stopping to film a 'nautch' or local dance, a thing of traditional, stylised movements and dress but enlivened by dark glasses which the actors fancy must make them resemble something out of Hollywood. Booth finished our appearance on the films with a manly handshake, and the intrepid climbers disappearing upward.

Sometimes, on these marches, I walked with Dikshya Man. One of his first questions, in the English with which he persisted, had been: "Do you know what I must do?"

"We thought *you* were going to tell *us* that, Dikshya Man. Aren't you supposed to stop us going up the wrong mountain?"

He had had a narrow escape with the gym shoes. When tried on at Pokhara, they proved at least three sizes too small. It turned out that his father had bought them, apparently without consulting his son's foot at all. Luckily he was able to exchange them at the bazaar, and now walked along, in shorts, carrying only a carefully rolled handkerchief with which he would mop his brow. He had brought, but inadvertently left at Pokhara, a book on the Army, which he intended to join. But as it was by Lieutenant-General Lord Weeks and concerned the organisation of General Staffs, Charles had brought him down to earth by describing the workings of a section and platoon. His other great interest was in philosophy and theology. Two of his remarks remained classics of the expedition: "What I want to know is, why has man come into this light?" And once, after being away for the afternoon: "I have been gossiping with an anchorite."

We climbed through haze to Ghandrung, sited among its bare terraces over two thousand feet above the Modi. It was the largest place we passed, and at first sight resembled a Sherpa village. David and I walked into it from camp. The houses stood in rows, neatly rectangular, built of smallish stones with big squares of slate-type stone for tiles, and small square windows. They were in tiers, with courtyards between on which barley was already being threshed with long sticks. An old man, looking up at the black clouds over the mountains ahead, told us not to go up there now, until all the barley was done. Why not wait till the monsoon, and then go up?

That was as far as I got, with my halting Urdu. But back in camp Jimmy had had a visitation from the headman, who had issued the same warning. He had not been very convincing, perhaps partly because Ghandrung depends for much of its prosperity on the Gurkha recruitment of which Jimmy is in charge. A promise was made that we would do our best to be tactful with the gods, whose sanctuary this is.

I was reminded forcibly that I had written a novel, *The Gods Are Angry*, in which the situation of a forbidden mountain and a party attempting it occurs. Sticky things happen to that party, and I hoped that they would not happen to us. But I had the same feeling now as when writing the novel, that there is an almost bridgeless gap between the true Oriental's way of looking at mountains, the abodes of fear and awe, and that of the eager Westerner, to whom it is almost sacrilege *not* to go scrambling up them just as fast as he can climb. That is partly why the Sherpas are interesting: in some measure they bridge the gap. Buddhists, they will yet eat meat and share the tins. Orientals, they have sometimes—Tenzing, for instance—the Westerner's ambition to stand upon the top, and are even helping to infuse that ambition into India. The Japanese, I suppose, have something of the same attitude, as well as the organising skill to realise their projects. But they have always, to my mind, stood well outside the main line of Eastern thought.

One thing that endeared us to the inhabitants was our medical service. A fine row of patients appeared, and I had plenty to give them. I found it a peculiarly satisfying trade to practise; Sganarelle himself could not have administered with more assurance. The chief trouble was eyes, and sometimes stomachs. For the former I squirted ointment, for the latter I had an assortment of pills. Everybody seemed happy, and I had the consolation of being in the next village before the complaints came. There were a few cases of terrible ulcers and mis-set limbs, for which I could do little but advise the hospital at Pokhara, a long journey as it seemed to these home-bound people.

Ghandrung faces straight into the Modi gorge, up which we would take three days from Chomrong, the last village. In the early morning light it was easy to sympathise with the belief that these mountains are sacred, the basin they enclose a sanctuary. From here Machapuchare looked once more like a fish-tail (Plate 8); for this view was almost diametrically opposite to the view from Annapurna IV (Frontispiece). The first sun touched the snow edge between the two summits with delicate pink. Below, the shadowed walls plunged in one frightening drop to the little hills. They looked cold, ice-bound, too impersonal even to be hostile. We lay in our sleeping-bags clicking away with cameras, in that pitiful attempt that humans feel obliged to make to capture the uncapturable.

Chomrong was not far off: a series of ins and outs, ups and downs and round the fields towards Ganesh, 23,607 feet, which with its 22,000-foot satellite Hiunchuli is the left-hand guardian of the sanctuary gates. Here we left the land of terraces and came into the land of trees: pine and deodar, rhododendron and Himalayan oak. Chomrong (about 6,000 feet), set among the woods above a tributary of the Modi, seemed to us the ideal of both climate and scenery. Its views are perfectly balanced: the broad snows of Ganesh to the left, to the right the single, aloof tower of Machapuchare. Below, the deep gorges give shadow to contrast with the woods that cling dizzily above. And the little village of Gurung houses nestles into the scene as if the same designer had painted the whole picture.

The locals came up, small and friendly with their round-faced women, the very type of the Gurkha. Jimmy was clearly at home here; one could imagine him retired in this valley, perhaps in a little house above the village. The evening was stormy; a presage of continual bad weather in the afternoons, had we known it. We crouched over our curry and rice under umbrellas. But the next morning dawned brilliant, waking us with that sense of well-being at which one looks back, later, and kicks one-self for not having realised how good it was. To roll over and drink tea in the sunrise, to get up and stroll across to the noisy little stream for a wash, grinning back at the coolies as they build their cheerful fires; to eat porridge, talking of this and that, perhaps of London theatres or mutual friends, looking up and around and wondering at it all but not daring to say much except:

"Peach of a day."

"Yes. Probably bust again this afternoon."

Then to watch the Sherpas doing the hard work of rolling up the tents, Ang Nyima chuckling that deep, rather lewd chuckle of his, Tashi pulling straps with an air of authority. Finally to pick up one's own light sack, assured of a pleasant stretch of the legs, an appetite, and more sun, starlight and companionable talk at the day's end. Such are the luxuries of existence.

Of the three days up the gorge, only the first was in fact pleasant. It took us up a reasonable path skirting the hill-side, through pine and rhododendron, to a patch of open grass at about 7,500 feet known as Kuldighar. A big, beautifully coloured bird had been caught here in a primitive gin: an Indian tragopan pheasant, and it made the dinner. On the second day we had to descend to bamboo country, near the river. The 'path', used by venturesome shepherds during the monsoon, all but disappeared. David, suffering badly from dysentery, missed it and must have found himself almost in the Modi's bed. He and I ended by bringing up a depressed rear—trip, stumble, umbrella catch, climb over fallen rhododendron, trip again, and the broken bamboos as sharp as knives. How they got sheep through this stuff! Clouds were lowering when, at 3.15 p.m., we reached a little stone structure four feet high, now decorated with three of our gay marker flags. This was the 'shrine' which marked the entrance to the Sanctuary. Beyond this point we were not allowed to take eggs or chicken, and the low caste coolies had had to be dismissed at Chomrong. Soon it began to rain.

We toiled on, feeling cold now in our shorts, tripping over wet boulders and snow patches. I began to feel an incipient diarrhoea, perhaps in sympathy. I hated the whole valley, and Machapuchare too. The camp site of Hinko is an enormous cave overhang, beyond which our tents were perched on little platforms dug out of the steep turf. Rainclouds hid our mountain, directly opposite. It was 5 p.m., and as we climbed at last into the big tent and sleeping-bags I felt uncomfortably like Rousseau's Rich Man; for there among the boulders were the coolies in their pitiful shawls, trying to coax fire out of nothing for their meagre chapatties.

About half the coolies, very understandably, did not want to go farther. The morning of the 24th was fine again, but a cold reminder that we were nearly 10,000 feet up. The valley-side opposite, which we had seen as vertical slabs disappearing into the mist and draped with daring conifers, revealed itself now as tier upon tier of towering rock buttresses. The one facing us we christened the Dru, from its likeness to the west side of the Dru above Chamonix. But it was only a feature in the great mountainside which wandered up, from the river below, to the silvery fish-tail 13,000 feet above our heads.

Sulphaguanadine was working wonders with David's insides, and I had now started the four-day course. But the sun came late here, and we did not want the coolies to start in shadow. They looked miserable, huddled over minute fires with all their nondescript garments draped about them. Twenty-seven however volunteered to come on, return to Hinko and carry the remaining loads next day. We started in the sunshine soon after 9 a.m.

The gorge, which had been fiercely steep-sided, now opened out. Its more level bed was still overhung by cliffs, but these kept their distance. Very soon we were on avalanche snow, great boulders of it down a gully, then on almost continuous patches which gave no rest to the coolies' feet. I remembered the Dhotiyals having difficulty in Garhwal; and was astonished to see how our Pokharis, who presumably never experienced really cold weather, went hopping barefoot across the blocks and, later, through the drifts. For there was no doubt that winter was very late this year. Great banks of old snow lay around, and more started to fall. We hurried on.

A line of old moraine, towards the left, led up through the last wretched bamboos and rhododendron. Jimmy pointed to his Base Camp site of 1956; what should have been grassy alp was now gentle névé backed by mysterious, dripping cliffs. We entered a small valley between a moraine and the hill-side, and followed what should have been a stream. The snow fell faster, the coolies came slower. Just after midday we arrived at a patch of bare snow and powdered dwarf juniper, in the ablation valley and just under the gentle side of the moraine which bounds the South-East Annapurna Glacier: our Base Camp, about 13,000 feet.

The first move was to cram windproofs over shivering knees and get the tents up. Through the falling snow, at last, the coolies loomed, their ragged blankets covering whatever they could cover. To our immense relief, after a cigarette and a sit-down with their feet on packing-

Base Camp in April, looking north up the gorge

Annapurna I, from its Sanctuary

In Gardyloo Gully

cases, they still agreed to go back to Hinko and return next day, for a handsome bonus. Admittedly their feet are tough as hide; once, when Knobbly-Knees complained of a cut, I had great difficulty in getting at it through the layers of leathery skin. Even so it was a stout effort, for the unknowns of lowering cliff and falling snow must have had their effect on morale. They had never seen anything like this before.

The most comforting tent was the big mess tent, supplied by Roger. If you have snow every afternoon, it is much pleasanter to grumble at it in the upright position, and in company. This was quickly erected and the others scattered around; while Dhanbahadur and the Sherpas rigged the kitchen tarpaulin under a most bleak-looking rock, and started on the tea.

The least at home in his surroundings was poor Dikshya Man. He had not really enjoyed the march, and the villagers seemed to speak a different dialect. To encourage him, we had pictured banks of fragrant primula on which he would lie while we climbed the mountain. Reality was disappointing. Moreover he now only had one book, an American work with the title: *Hope for the Troubled: a genial warm-hearted guide to those who are psychologically disturbed.* Over this he brooded in his tent, and made a word list to assist his studies. This came out in the evening.

"What is schizophrenia, please?"

Unanswerable question—at any rate in words of one syllable. That night, after a snowy supper of soup and

E

our usual rice mixture, he was receiving some instruction from Charles about the soldier's qualifications.

"You have to be practical too."

Dikshya Man was impressed with this. "Yes, one must be practical." He stumped off to bed, and that night badly burnt the entrance flap of the tent he was using, by upsetting his lighted candle.

Next morning, like almost all mornings, was brilliant. From the moraine top, 200 yards above camp, we had a clear view of our problem. (Plate 3).) The Modi rumbled away a good 700 feet below; from there to the summit was about the same in height as from Everest Base Camp to the top of Everest. There would be (comparatively speaking) no breathing difficulties, but a good deal of tedious carrying.

From about 14,500 to 18,000 feet there lay a stretch of easy-looking glacier, if we could get to it. But the whole lower part of the mountain, from the Modi, was guarded by vertical cliffs—the ones that we had been admiring on the way up. In only one place were they broken: a deep, snake-like gully, rather like Pier's Ghyll on Lingmell, bit into the mountain's breast. Jimmy had christened it Gardyloo Gully. Snow-filled, it disappeared round a corner and we could not see whether it had an exit; but there seemed no other way. This was the first of Machapuchare's many improbabilities.

In the upper regions, the north and slightly higher of the twin summits showed as an enormous triangle, almost a horn. Its curling left edge continued to a sharp minor point, christened the Rock Gendarme; thence by a long ridge, with many ups and downs, to a northerly col about a mile and a half away. This ridge had of course been invisible from the south. It might be very sharp, but about half-way along was a big rocky hump, the 'Rock Buttress'. We reckoned that the first need was to explore Gardyloo and from its top to reach the North Col. We might be able to get along the ridge; if it was too sharp, we could perhaps drop off the other side, and reach one of the snowfields. In 1950 Jimmy had seen and photographed this angle from Annapurna II (Frontispiece). Once reached, they had seemed to lead up easily to the final snow and ice steepness, which we knew to lie just round the corner from that soaring left-hand edge.

From our moraine top, one was well placed to admire the great vertical limestone cliffs that bounded Gardyloo to left and right. Later, when the snows melted, waterfalls of four or five hundred feet would go cascading from their tops, each spout of water losing itself as it fanned out on the slow descent. I felt the force of Goethe's poem far more strongly here than at Lauterbrunnen, for which it was written. Left of Gardyloo one could see the river bed disappearing into what was really the upper reach of the Modi gorge, whence it descended cold from the glaciers which we were to explore later under the rim. Annapurna III itself was invisible, unless you climbed a little way up the ablation valley behind, and if you did that you also saw well a most shapely peak on the ridge between Annapurna III and the Fish's Tail. It was christened by us the Ober Gabelhorn, from its resemblance, and was a thing of fairy ice ridges.

Looking north, over the indescribable rubble and dirt of the South-East Annapurna Glacier, you were faced with a series of blunt rock buttresses divided by grassy gullies—the lower reaches, in fact, of Tent Peak (see map page 15). Somewhere up here, we knew, the Chomrong shepherds get their flocks to graze during the monsoon, right over the shoulder of Tent Peak, and how they do it remains a mystery. The crossing of the glacier alone must be a pretty problem. Behind that and to the left lay the immense bulk of Annapurna I, best seen from up the valley (Plate 10a). On this side it drops its southeast face sheer some 12,000 feet to the glacier. The French, of course, climbed it in 1950 from the other side, and no part of their route was ever visible to us.

If we looked fairly due west, as we often did because the weather came from there, it was up our very gentle ablation valley, formed on the right by the easy side of the glacier moraine, on the left by the first slopes of Hiunchuli, satellite to Ganesh. Ganesh itself could be seen straight ahead, as headpiece to the valley, a towering bastion of ice. But as can be seen from Plate 12 it is a mountain of many summits, and we were never really positive which was the highest. Between it and Annapurna I stretched a long ridge, interrupted by one surprising point which we called the Finger (just visible on the left of Plate 10a). The only other feature of special note, led up to by gradually steepening gullies of rhododendron and then rock, was that shoulder of Hiunchuli which directly overlooks the Modi, and which we called the Cloudmaker. Here, on the brightest of mornings, an innocent little puff of cotton wool would first hang playfully, the sure presage of snow or hail.

Looking down from the moraine you would observe Base Camp friendly and colourful at your feet. The tents, varying according to the stage we had reached on the mountain, stood out yellow or orange or green, toys that contrasted pleasantly with the grandeur around. Dhanbahadur might be vanishing under the wicker and tarpaulin awning of the kitchen; and there would be Tashi, doing efficient things with ropes, or the bright red sweaters of Jimmy and Roger, or simply Dikshya Man in stately pose, his arms folded, contemplating the infinite.

Our very first need was to acquire some sort of acclimatisation. On the 25th, while the coolies were appearing bravely with the last loads, Jimmy stayed in camp to greet and dismiss them. The rest of us walked westward up the ablation valley, towards Ganesh. The walking was easy, about an hour and a half over snow which should at this season have been grass, until we came to the moraine's end and looked down on the desolate jumble of boulder and dirty ice which styles itself grandly the South-East Annapurna Glacier. Cloud had descended; but next day we all repeated the dose, and from the moraine's end climbed leftwards up slopes towards Hiunchuli. In our overweening pride we were convinced that Ganesh or Hiunchuli could be added at a later stage.

But the snow came down, despite a fine frosty morning, and blotted out the hoped-for view, both of the glacier system we were on and of everything else. At about 15,500 feet we turned round, amid dramatic thunder that was to become a monotonous everyday accompaniment over the next weeks. Roger's axe sizzled slightly.

But tomorrow, and this seemed the important point, for the first time in the history of the world somebody was going to set foot on one of the world's most beautiful mountains. And thanks to those twenty-seven coolies, we were nicely set to try and reach its top.

CHAPTER FIVE

Of Mountain Obstacles and
Human Infirmity

Remote, serene, and inaccessible.
—SHELLEY

IT IS AN ANNOYING HABIT of many mountains that they start with a downhill path, meaning an uphill path at the end of the day. Of this group Machapuchare is an honourable member. The Modi roared below, but on the 27th we had to reach it down gentle snow at first, then moraine, then slippery boulders which gave a sudden, welcome view of the bridge built by Ang Nyima the autumn before. A few big birch logs cast across and lashed together; that was all, but it was enough. We were over the tumbling grey stream and walking along, a quarter of a mile or so on frozen snow patches, at the base of vertical cliffs. Then we were at the start of Gardyloo Gully, seven hundred feet below Base.

We walked up it—all except Charles, who had caught the stomach bug—with the diffidence of intruders. As we rose the sides steepened, the limestone cliffs overhung behind their lace-work of ice curtains. Occasionally small rock and ice boulders showed that things do some-times fall down, and there had been a big mud slide here in June; but on all our ascents and descents we never saw anything seriously in motion. About twenty yards wide, the gully turned and twisted until at last it became clear that there *was* going to be an exit: an even, rounded slope on the right which would lead steeply but fairly on to easier ground. Having gained this, we paused. The height was only some 15,000 feet, and juniper showed through a thick snow covering as we plodded leftward, towards a great black knob of rock which we had picked out for the site of Camp One. It jutted boldly above us, a little way under a much bigger, triangular patch of rock which had been christened the 'Rognon' from its Alpine resemblance. By the time we arrived, 1 p.m., a charac-teristic Welsh winter day had set in, snowing hard. We huddled over a packed lunch in all the accustomed attitudes, then sped down easily to the ice overhangs of Gardyloo for a sheltered pipe. The first improbability had been surmounted.

28th April was given to preparation. Jimmy and Charles would go up towards Ganesh, for apart from our desire to have a look at these two great peaks, there was work to be done. In order to qualify for a grant from the Everest Foundation we had, in common with many other adventurers, pocketed our purist pride and bowed the head to science, volunteering to do survey work with the assistance of the Royal Geographical Society. The scientific proviso is perhaps not a bad down-to-earth for those, like myself, who tend to be high-minded about their mountaineering. On this expedition it was vaguely pleasant to think that we were adding our mite to geographical science by correcting a big error on the Indian Survey map of the area. Jimmy was far the most expert in that field; from the angles he took and from many photographs, he later produced a most competent sketch map—the one solid fruit of all our labours—which may some day be incorporated in one of the bigger maps. My own contribution, apart from photographs on Fluted Peak, was a daily meteorological report which I kept for the ultimate benefit of New Delhi. It ran with monotonous regularity something like this: "Cloudless morning, sharp frost. 11 a.m. cumulus from S.W. . . . . 1 p.m. snow . . . hail. . . ." I hope somebody has found it helpful.

Roger, David and I would go up and reconnoitre the North Col. This division of forces worried Dikshya Man at first, since he had at last grasped the central fact that his main job was to keep us all on the same mountain—the one we had paid for. The longest excursion he made from Base was when he followed Jimmy three hundred yards to reason with him. I hope he was finally convinced that our permission covered survey of the basin, with the attainment of points needed for that end. Unbeknown to himself, however, Dikshya Man was playing a more useful role than his official one. In a party like ours, where everybody is sweetly reasonable and never a cross word, it is possible for a certain keen edge of humour and temper to be lost, from want of grinding. *Mountain Craft* remarks that a younger member who does not mind being laughed at or abused can lighten the whole party's mood. Our liaison officer minded neither, since he did not know when they were happening, and we came to regard him with something like affection.

A long patch of brown, snow-pressed grass had appeared. One primula, a *Denticulata*, peeped bravely out. In the hill-side a little stream allowed a wash, and the men about town, Jimmy and Roger, shaved. Charles started by shaving, but later followed David and myself who remained shaggy. Wispy clouds high in heaven forebore, today, to summon the big battalions. Things could be spread out. Birch stakes were cut, and their tops looped with nylon; bamboos had marker flags tied to them. Manila rope, tents, pitons, food, nylon, everything was stacked. For tomorrow we would have up all four Sherpas with the first relay for the mountain. Two of them, next day, would join the others, two come up again with further loads to help along the slow process generally known as 'build-up'. By evening all was ready.

* * *

We were late starting. It was 8.40 a.m., breakfast had been late coming and I had felt that 'Rabbity' urge to be busy which I mistrust in myself. We were all carrying over forty lbs, the Sherpas over fifty, by the time we started the tedious business of going downhill in order to go up. But the sun shone, there was a crispness in the air and on the snow surface as we plodded across to the gully's foot. Up it we went, very slowly, resting generously to "wait for the Sherpas". Surprisingly, it was Roger who lagged this time. He had a reputation for always carrying more and going faster than anybody else.

Hope springs eternal, and yesterday we had said: "Ah, the weather's changing." But an evil dragon-head of frothy cloud, a regular visitor later, came poking its nose up the gorge, round Hiunchuli's rocky shoulder, and by 11 a.m. it was snowing. By 2 p.m. it was snowing harder, as we struggled to pitch two tents end to end on the rock knob. Tashi was with us. In his philosophy it was a cardinal tenet that no sahib knew how to select a camp site, and he was soon predicting that these tents would be blown off by the most modest breath of wind. For the first of many times we tried to arrange wet sacks, wet boots, wet Li-Los inside a wet tent with the minimum of discomfort. Roger arrived, coming very slowly. His feet felt chilled, he said, as if by frostbite. But that was absurd, it was so warm. A queer kind of mountain sickness? It seemed so.

Roger had done his job on the food skilfully. There is nothing that makes a man feel so much at home as to lie in a sleeping-bag sipping tea, his other hand clasped around a sweet biscuit. We had three sorts, Family Assorted, Digestive and Ginger, the pride of their makers and each popular in its turn. For supper we ate a 'hoosh' which became our standard meal on the mountain: dehydrated meat bar shredded and boiled, with soup, potato, raisins, nuts and anything else there happened to be thrown in. A delicious mixture—at least at first. Then we lay and listened to the wind, and wondered whether Tashi would be right after all.

The wind died (it seldom reappeared in force) leaving a clear, cold dawn. At 5 a.m. porridge started to heat. Roger, the chef, was slow to move but said that he would come on. Today's job was to reconnoitre a site for Camp Two, which would be carried tomorrow with the help of the two Sherpas, due back with fresh loads. Only Dikshya Man would be still at Base, communing, presumably, with Dhanbahadur about the intricacies of the psyche.

Across the basin Annapurna I reared up its 12,000-foot south-east face, gigantic, dominant, but not beautiful. Today, as often, a high wisp of cirrus draped its head, developing into a regular 'sausage' which was usually ominous. By 6.40 we were off, making for the top of the Rognon nearly 1,000 feet higher. The snow was heavy, we changed leads. At the top Roger said he would come on slowly; and looking back, later, we saw him lying full length against his rucksack. It seemed strange, but no more, and our dull minds were absorbed by the immediate problem.

This consisted mainly of putting one foot in front of the other. Above the Rognon the snow was nearly knee-deep. Slowly we were approaching the steep upper tiers of the mountain, under which ran an obvious broad terrace of glacier; but to reach this we must bear right, avoiding a primitive crevasse area, then back left. Both operations took a long time. Soon after the sun hit us it became very hot, and we blessed the early start. We took it in turns, and I remember wondering eagerly when David would call up "My turn"; or, when he was leading, dreading the moment when pride would compel me to do the same. At about 11 a.m. some way along the terrace, we dumped ourselves and loads down and agreed that this was about as far as the Sherpas would manage. Then we lay and sunbathed, at about 18,000 feet.

Back at camp, in the early afternoon, there was no sign of life—or tea. In his overheated tent Roger lay fast asleep, his sweater and boots still on. It must be the effect of soneryl and codeine combined, we thought. We brewed tea and lemonade, for the unacclimatised are very thirsty, and sat outside. The sun still shone, this time through a heat-haze, and on the flat below we could pick out Tashi and Ang Tsering coming up. They too needed tea. Then they pitched their tent prudently and uncomplainingly in the snow alongside our knob. It was an evening of quiet and of distant views.

The First of May. It is extraordinary how much longer a camp takes to leave if you have to pack it up. "Roger still sick, nausea and feverish, so stays, his tent to come up tomorrow," my diary records callously. At the time it never occurred either to ourselves or to the Sherpas that anyone should stay with him. It was a case of altitude

sickness, nothing more. We were not off till 9.10 a.m.
the four of us; and with forty-lb. loads, despite the tracks,
the going was hot and heavy. At the one patch of ice we
cut big steps. We stopped little but went on wearily,
raising foot after slow foot, like machines that are running
down. Sometimes we sucked sweets. At our dumping
place of yesterday we very reluctantly decided to go on;
for here, on the open terrace, playful snowballs tended to
come spinning down from the gullies above. And they
might get larger. But 300 yards on, a triangle of rock,
built into the snow, would give clear protection. It
seemed a long way. For my part I could only summon
resolution by dumping my load to make the tracks, then
returning for it while the others pitched Camp Two.
Soon David and I were alone.

*　*　*

Looking back on them now, I see that the six days of this
reconnaissance should have been among the happiest of
the whole journey. We had the best weather, though we
did not appreciate it at the time, we enjoyed climbing
with each other and we were confronted with an in-
triguing problem. But in memory the days are clouded.
At the back of our minds was Roger, for one thing. We
were not acclimatised, and the effort of camp chores, the
blocking of nostrils and bad tastes in the mouth, all
seemed more irritating than later. Also, I think, we were
both impressed and depressed by the enormous walls and

spires above us. Later we accepted them, as one accepts anything after a time.

We did enjoy meals, however. David was usually chef —very careful, which is a good thing in chefs, and patient. We delighted in putting everything we had into the mixture. By 6.30 supper was finished. A light mist, which had sprinkled snow since early afternoon, vanished now, leaving Annapurna I in all his sunset splendour. Soon after dark, for darkness comes early here, we slept.

On the glacier terrace that forms a base to the steep ice furrows or 'flutings' under the north ridge, it was crisp in the early morning as it is at dawn in the Alps. We always put off getting up to the last moment, cooking and eating our porridge in bed to fortify us against the dread moment. Today there was some inducement to be off, in the brisk air and the exciting thought of seeing 'over the top'. One or two giant crevasses went the same way as ourselves and gave out under a twisting rib of snow that descends, really, from a big snow hump (about 20,000 feet) on the right of the col (Plate 3). The snow, or snow-ice as we called it, was fairly steep, too steep to walk up even in crampons. Each step needed two or three blows with the adze of the axe. Scoop, scoop, step; scoop, scoop, step. They gave the illusion, at least to the cutter, that rapid progress was being made. In reality it was very slow. This rib gave out in a snowy bay under a huge split block of ice. We could have continued straight up, to the Hump, but decided on the col, which was lower (19,500 feet) and now appeared some way to the left again, beyond the bay. A long plod over, and the climb started. Here the flutings lay back more gently than farther to the right; a chip or two from time to time sufficed. But it seemed a long pull, our bodies weary and breath short, before we reached a crest which, quite suddenly, had nothing at all beyond. For, over an immediate cornice which we dared not tread, black mist welled up to greet us from the Seti Khola. On that side the ridge seemed to drop straight into the abyss.

But it was the view southward, slowly being swallowed by mist, that held us. It is approximately that of Plate 11a, but from higher up. No mountain scene has ever awed me with greater sense of the beautiful and inaccessible. Even Ama Dablam near Everest looks heavy in comparison with the feathery ridge that raced away from under our feet, over the Snow Hump and then, twisting in its course, along to two soaring triangles of ice. These, on later and closer view, turned out to be the two apparently insignificant rises in the crest seen from Base Camp. After them, ever sharper and hung with cornices in each direction, the edge soared up to the so-called 'Rock Buttress', now a 21,000-foot peak in its own right. Trembling, the eye travelled on to the still higher and sharper 'Rock Gendarme'. And behind that, vignetted against the blue by wisps of dusky cloud, the final wedge rose shadowy and unbelievable to the summit. On the right a clean-cut rock edge dropped sheer towards the Modi; on the left a steepening spiral of giant ice steps

Rock Buttress, summit and Rock Gendarme from way up to North Col. Camp Three was on ice bulges directly below Rock Buttress

Roger Chorley starting down, 9th May

Sherpas on the little serac of Camp Three. Ganesh behind

held the morning sun. Compared with that vision the Matterhorn would have looked crude, the peerless Weisshorn a flattened lump.

Some humans see very little beyond the next step, and this is a fortunate characteristic of those who visit the Himalaya. David and I did not worry overmuch about how we were to get up that. We gasped at it, made a mental note of the Snow Hump as an objective for to-morrow. From it we should get a closer view of the ridge, see the section which it was hiding and also, perhaps—vain hope—snowfields the other side. Then we turned to the important business of getting down. Far more than by the mountain, David was worried by a feeling of nausea, when he kicked toes into the slope and had to look down between his legs for the next kick. The lower steepness was "bloody but short" (diary). At last we were trudging hotly back across the glacier, to find the Sherpas returned with more loads. They bore also a note from Roger, saying that he had wanted to go up but thought it wiser to go down. It was.

Tea-time was always a good time. David is the ideal camp-companion, since he usually usurps the larger share of the work. He also smokes a pipe heavily, which is another companionable thing to do. Once, at about 15,000 feet, he was found smoking it while walking uphill. Over tea one could lie and read, free of worries. Supper was a more serious business, demanding concentration and excursions outside which became colder as the evening advanced. After supper we read a little by candle;

then lay looking up at the darkened tent roof, talking of this and that, till we dropped off.

The route for 3rd May was the same as to the col, as far as the split block. Then we must follow the steepening line of blunt ridge that led directly to the Snow Hump, about 1,500 feet above. Here again was snow-ice, needing for every step two or three blows from the axe. The zigzags seemed endless, the height gained at each glance round negligible. Surprising how slow it was. Chip, chip, chip, step; chip, chip, chip, step. David shouted up encouragingly that we had topped the North Col; but it seemed impossible. At about two-thirds height the angle steepened to ice, a long and disheartening job. Meanwhile the clouds were playing over the ridge above our heads. I suggested a traverse left, to hit the ridge at about our own height, thence back to the top. A long traverse, and bending to chip the steps made them more arduous. At the ridge we rested, breathless and curiously drained of strength, looking back at the col. Its eastern side, seen from here, was of literally overhanging rock, disappearing into the mist after the manner of the old Alpine prints. There followed the last half-hour up the ridge, as unpleasant as anyone could wish. The east-facing cornice was rotten to the touch, the slope in the west side steep. We scrabbled along crabwise, chipping still where necessary. David offered to take over. I kept up the groundless pride of one who had been in these parts before, and was supposed to be more used to altitude. Inwardly I abused myself for doing so. At 1 p.m., tired and dry-throated, we dragged ourselves on to the flat top of the Hump, after nearly six hours' hard going.

Mist had closed in, and we saw little but vignettes. What we did see, however, looked as bad as yesterday's view: hard climbing by Alpine standards, impossible for laden Sherpas. Whether from weariness or false optimism, we deposited here the 200 feet of manila rope in our sacks. They must be there still. We ate and drank, then turned to go down. The descent was a nightmare: nowhere excessively steep in itself, yet nowhere a place for a tired and unacclimatised body to risk slipping. We took it facing into the slope, kicking hard and digging the pick in too, desperately; rope length by rope length. This is one of the dreariest and thirstiest processes that I know. Our lips were caked, hands sweaty despite the cold snow. Kick—axe in—slither to stop—kick again, axe rammed hard—slither again. I rummaged for acid drops, which stayed the pangs for a while. David did not seem so badly hit. On the traverse more tedious steps must be cut, since the upward ones were too widely spaced. The lower zigzags seemed endless, till David at last spotted a gully of soft snow alongside, laborious with its great knee-deep holes, but easy. At last we were on the glacier.

Tiredness has a strange way of impressing beauty on an inward eye which opens when the other faculties have become incapable of receiving impression. I remember no scene better than that across the valley, a back-cloth to two small figures on a wide and weary plain. Across the great gulf which backed our disappearing foreground, black masses of cloud had been hanging. But through them, now, swords of light pierced to the blunt top of Hiunchuli, picking out its ridges in silver. Behind, Ganesh and the Annapurna ridge showed as suggestions rather than shapes in the darkness. And the swords of light came nearer, to touch us too with their comfort.

It was 5.30 p.m. when, after over ten hours on the mountain, we crawled into our tent. Tea first, then food. Then sleep. In that order. For once I did not even enjoy being tired.

* * *

The big mess tent seemed deserted, but Dikshya Man appeared to greet us. He had not been more than 300 yards from the camp, and was glad to see us again. But it was Roger we wanted to see. He came hobbling in on an ice-axe. His left leg gave him no help, he said, but he spoke little about it, facing the future stoically. We had tea together, and Dhanbahadur gave of his best, delicious bread such as I always associate with return to Base anywhere, along with the disappearance of bunged nose, dry throat, bad tastes in the mouth. Afterwards we lay luxuriously among the primulas (at last!), and I watched a marten playing among the rocks: a friendly, predatory creature to which we had become attached. Sometimes two of them appeared, leaving the traces of their gambols in the snow.

Next day Roger could not get up. His temperature

had risen to 102 the night before, but was now coming down. He did not complain of any pain, but his legs would not obey him. The miracle was that they had obeyed him sufficiently to allow the descent from Camp One; and even then it had taken him two hours to make the 700 feet up from the river. Now, it was terrible to see him squirm on his elbows, if he wanted something from the back of the tent. The disease must be polio, even if we had never met it before. Immobility was prescribed, while we kept looking up the ablation valley for the others, and were glad when they appeared soon after lunch. They had had a most strenuous time, for the Ganesh side seems to take most of the snowfall. They had camped twice on the glacier, and had reached—at about 19,500 feet—a point 500 feet short of the col between Ganesh and Hiunchuli. The former looked possible, they said, but would be a long job from our low Base Camp. They had taken important photographs.

The immediate concern was Roger. He was worried by an inability to perform the natural functions, and his arms and right leg felt weaker too. We determined to build a luxury latrine, on which he could spend the day if he liked. Everybody was glad to be doing something, however trivial, to help. The Sherpas competed in producing bigger and better boulders, and Dikshya Man topped the lot by heaving up something that would have graced Stonehenge. Curved birch logs completed the structure, on to which the patient was hoisted with ceremony and left in state.

But he must be taken down soon, and Jimmy made a plan. On the 7th Da Temba would be dispatched at top speed to order carriers from Chomrong and then go on to Pokhara, to the hospital of the British women. On the 9th the cortège would start down, led by Jimmy, who had the administrative arrangements at his finger-tips. A wise but very melancholy decision, since he himself would miss the greater part of the mountain. For the rest of us there were other things to be going on with. An article waited to be written by me, and a plan made for the next phase on the mountain. We had decided to abandon the col, and make an attempt to reach the ridge much nearer the summit; then either to go along it, if it had flattened at all, or to cross it. David and I had noticed independently that here the angle did not look prohibitively steep; and that about two-thirds way up there ran a line of big ice bulges. Now an ice bulge is a very uncomfortable object to be under, since it has a nasty habit of breaking away; but its top may just form a very flat and friendly camp site, and from these we could attack the last 700 feet or so to the ridge. Once again, therefore, as afternoon hail beat down upon the mess tent and thunder rumbled, we sat round on boxes working out the next stage of the attempt, which would also be the next stage of the build-up. (See map, page 15, for the route.)

On the 7th Tashi and Ang Tsering carried loads up to Camp One, to supplement the stores, mainly manila rope and ironmongery, already on the mountain. They were to continue to Two next day. We could see the tiny figures moving very slowly out of Gardyloo Gully opposite. That afternoon a real hurricane of hail hammered at the tents. By 9 p.m., when it stopped, the place looked much as when we had arrived, and the primulas nothing but forlorn little humps under the general blanketing. But the 8th dawned fine again, and after the usual packings and forgettings, the good-byes and the handshakes, the sadness of seeing Roger lie there in the sun for the last time, we were off. Jimmy came a little way down.

"Go for the top for heaven's sake. Don't wait for me."

A characteristic sentiment.

CHAPTER SIX

The Ways of Storms

Not seldom, clad in radiant vest,
Deceitfully goes forth the morn.
                                        —WORDSWORTH

IT STILL TOOK nearly five hours up to Camp One.
Before we arrived the snow had started but the sun shone
through it, as it was to do often, a great incandescent
circle. The tracks of Tashi and Ang Tsering went only a
few yards above camp; for the hail which had be-
laboured us at Base was stiffer up here, and they had
retired prudently, '*pour mieux sauter*' on the morrow. I
am not quite sure, apart from that, why they retired.
Tashi had certainly the determination to go on. Perhaps
he felt his responsibility. The Sherpas, three of them at
any rate, carried and climbed so well that one tended to
assume that they were also capable of bigger mountaineering decisions, as a British climber would be. In fact it was
natural, I suppose, for them to prefer having the decisions
made by us.

When the snow stopped we climbed out and dug away

Ice flutings and Rock Gendarme from Camp Three

Two climbers descending the east side of the Nick

Ice traverse below Camp Three

the loads, admiring the great waves of black cumulus topped with sun down the valley. "They'll be having it bad at Ghandrung," we said. And then we added: "They must be cursing us by now." We little realised that these storms are so local that Ghandrung had in fact been suffering a severe drought. When Jimmy reached it, he found the neighbouring lamas summoned to invoke *rain*. "*Tantum religio . . .*" he told them, but in his own words.

On the 9th Roger would be starting down, and it would be hot where he was going, but up here it was cold before the sun struck, and still shaded at 7.55 a.m. when we started, heavily laden. After 8.30 the sun warmed us, but my toes remained cold, for I had left my high-altitude boots up at Two. On the hot and stagnant bog of a glacier we appreciated Tashi's prudence of the day before; the tent, when we reached it, was buried under one and a half feet of snow. The idea of collapsing it was not a good one, as we were to find even more later on, and it took an hour and a half to get everything upright and the Primus going. Tea, with lemon or orange powder, was the favourite drink, a drink of which a thirsty man could never tire. After that, supper, and an upset with the Primus. This was a not infrequent disaster just now, since the burner on this particular stove resolutely refused to screw down into its proper position below the supports. Thus for each meal a delicate balancing act was needed. During the whole expedition I remember six or seven upsets, and it is a proof of friendship that these were accepted with resignation (the responsibility being about evenly divided). The stew, scraped out of wind-proofs or sleeping-bags, returned to the pot.

We reckoned on a week of reconnoitring, step-cutting, rope-fixing and the like before the ridge could be reached at 20,700 feet; in fact the whole operation took nine days. This first day David and I climbed the couloir and ribs just right of camp, then straight up. Over Annapurna I the sausage had developed, a great balloon, broad and long and menacing. After a while we took to cutting up a snow-ice rib, but found that we had come too far to the right. We were directly under the huge slanting layer of black rock which gives the Rock Buttress its only title to its name. But below the left-hand bottom end of the layer, up to our left, we could see that a gully or gullies ran up out of sight between Buttress and ice bulges. If we could strike that gully, work up it a little and then traverse left, out on to the top of the bulges, we might have hope of a camp site. After agreeing that there was no point in trying to work across from where we were today, but that we should start on the left, the way we would be going tomorrow, we descended.

Charles had brought up the three remaining Sherpas and a gift of bread from Dhanbahadur. There had been some difficulty in getting going from Camp One, since Ang Nyima had an arrangement with the men of Chomrong to send up *rakshi* (spirit) whenever a party ascended. The men had duly arrived on the 8th, though very late and with bleeding feet. An ex-Gurkha *subadar*, who led them, had shot a *jharal* (Himalayan *tahr*), a beast similar to an ibex but with much shorter horns. These men are inveterate hunters, and they had spent four happy but fruitless hours looking for it. Anyway, they had brought Ang Nyima's *rakshi*, and the celebration had continued to Camp One, slowing down the early-morning start. The three now went down once more, leaving Charles installed in a second tent and promising to return with a last load in two days' time.

Once again, on the 11th, a sense of excitement spurred cold hands into activity. If this line proved impossible, we might have to give up. Before 5 o'clock Primuses sputtered and we were looking doubtfully at the 'sausage', which had spread to some of the other summits. By 6.30 we were away, up the long gully to the left this time, in wide zigzags that grew narrower gradually as the gully grew steeper. This 'Great Gully' must have been over 1,000 feet high, and its left-hand branch gave out steeply on a sloping shoulder which formed both the pedestal of the Rock Buttress and the right wall of the gully separating us from the ice bulges. Charles, throwing his heart into the job of cine-photographer, took his life in his hands to go traversing right, fix his tripod at an impossible angle against the slope and film our antics on the snow shoulder.

The lower section of the bulges plunged down in great overhanging walls directly opposite; we were still over 300 feet below any possible line of crossing. At about half width a series of steep snow ribs split the gully, divided by stretches of green ice. The angle was high; the ice

needed large, cautious steps. It turned out as hard ice as
I have met, though I could not swear that it was that
special 'Himalayan' ice of which Frank Smythe has
written. It has always seemed to me that tough ice is
tough ice, whether you meet it in Nepal or on the Brenva
side of Mont Blanc. The ice took us to one rib; this too
was steep, and seemed in an uncomfortable way to be no
more than glued on to the iron-hard substance below. It
would be safe with fixed ropes, now. But after a fortnight's sun? We crawled gingerly up our chipped steps,
250 feet up two lines of rib. At that point the bulges
opposite showed an enormous ice cave hung with fairy
icicles; and beside it, to our huge delight, a line of easy
snow leading out to the edge, the bulge top—and a camp
site.

Jordan still flowed between, in the form of a green band
of vertically set ice, then a snow traverse. But it would
have taken more than that to stop my present elation.
The ice threw me well out of balance, but was firm enough
to bear handholds cut in it. A few steps only, then the
snow. With gasps of relief we plumped down in the
shade and admired the blues and grey-greens of our
grotto, the crystal bubbles that seemed to plunge into im-
measurable depths, the little stalactites that hung and
dripped from the polished vault. But this was no place for
a camp, and after rest we plodded out to the edge. Up
here the bulges' angle was easing, but there remained one
big, snow-mantled *sérac* to round. At its back was a
small, fairly level space, rather like that of Camp Seven on

Everest. We had had enough, and our throats were dry. Here in the hot sun of midday we sat and reckoned this the ideal spot for Camp Three. Above, a vertical ice wall gave shelter, but if one went down and up to the *sérac* top (fairly amenable on this side) and peered round it, the general angle looked none so bad and the crest of the North Ridge itself not more than 700 feet above our heads.

It was a feature of that year's bad weather that its approach had always about it the reputed innocence of the lamb. A few wisps of cirrus, perhaps, and the early morning sausage, of course, but these disappeared as the sun rose dazzling in a cloudless sky—or almost cloudless, for a happy, woolly sort of cloud sea usually played over the southern valleys. Nobody could have called that 'dragon-head' of cloud that came nosing up the Modi ominous. And then, suddenly . . . This time Charles had been filming some rope-fixing on the traverse, for we had put pitons into the ice and linked it with 100 feet of rope to the grotto. The sun shone, steamy coils of mist wreathed us from below. Now we were fixing 200 feet of rope down the ribs, myself enjoying mightily the sensation of hammering in a tough birch stake and then sliding down on a rope fixed to it. The hail started almost without our noticing it.

For about twenty minutes I was too absorbed in the work to worry. After that it did seem that the upward steps had become strangely invisible. I was not really worried at this everyday visitation; but we must move quickly. The last rope we left dangling and made off across the lower snow traverse (the ice could be avoided) to the top of Great Gully; then down that, facing in. David was now in front, kicking hard, but his steps were filled in with the slithering, endless pellets by the time the next man reached them. Through the blinkers of my hood I saw nothing but a grey, sugary few feet and the tumbling stream above that made the whole place look alive. Then the slope eased, we turned outwards, clumsily stumbling for hold below the cascade. I thought of the haven of the little tents, and blessed them when they showed up square and solid in that dim, indefinite world.

I had also been thinking about the bread. It is curious, this need of the human being to have something cosy to look forward to, however simple. This is why Antarctic explorers tuck away sweets to be produced as a morale-booster. After due debate we decided to have the bread now, with honey, before the tea brewed. This was as well, because as we ate it, and as the hail pattered on, I kept noticing the tent on my slopeward side pushing me in. To keep my place I had to keep up a constant tension. By the time Charles, from his tent, was shouting "Tea up!" we were shouting back:

"Well, the slope's coming down!"

We needed the energy of that bread and honey.

The slope did indeed seem to be on its way down. It had looked such a sheltered place, under the rock triangle; but we had reckoned without the smooth pellets which have no cohesion to them and which now, with a gentle hiss, came streaming down from the slopes alongside. The whole weight of the mountain-side was bent on pushing the little tent until it broke; while at each entrance sly pellets came slithering through the cracks, as if to take the enemy from the rear. On floor or sleeping-bag they melted damply, adding their mite of discomfort. I remember saying: "This is a crisis"; then David scrambled out while I tried to push back the weight. A vain hope, and I scrambled out to join him. The smothered tent, an Everest Edgington, was riding it out bravely. True, the pellets were very light; but there were plenty of them. In their myriads they continued to hiss gently down and over, down and over. And the sky was still black with more.

The time was 4 o'clock, and for nearly three hours we bucketed away with shovel, plates, mugs, anything that came to hand. Charles, a military man, set about it in a business-like way by digging a channel above, to divert the stream. This seemed to work, for a time. What I lacked in skill I made up for in desperate energy; since the prospect of losing one tent added strength to the arm. And we needed it, for as one plateful disappeared, so another poured down to take its place.

By 6.30 p.m. the storm was easing off. Charles and David got the stoves going, I floundered on for a while, tripping over buried guys, fumbling after buried equipment. In the end only one mug was lost...

It was a restless night, preluded by a spilling of cocoa (my fault this time) which added to the wetness of our bags. Besides this I had the impression in my damp dreams that my back was supporting the whole weight of the mountain above. For the slope continued to slide, in bits and pieces, and more hail fell. A bleak morning lowered dully, and with dry throats and a general air of woe we hurried to dig out a platform below Charles's tent. Then the upper tent had to be dug out: a long job, since the guys were deep-covered by pellets, while the pegs and base of the tent had been iced in by ten days of sun and frost. David worked inside, collecting impedimenta and wiping up cocoa mess. I dug and shifted while Charles in his tent cooked. The move was just about finished when more hail and snow descended, and we lay awkwardly, knees bent and necks awry, feeling rather cold and miserable, discussing a move of the whole camp over brews of coffee. To 'dry things out' seemed a good excuse for keeping the Primus going. We should perhaps have tried to shift today; but a few steps outside in waist-deep softness showed that it would be a formidable job. And the mountain would need a day or two anyway, we said, to get rid of this fresh mantle.

At about 1 p.m. the hail stopped, a weak sun shone through. We congratulated ourselves that this was not the Karakoram, where such storms have a habit of going on for days. Charles was the first to climb out and start in again on his channel. We followed half-heartedly, but warmed with the work. By tea-time the storm clouds had withdrawn their black battalions down the valley, and from the sea that stretched between ourselves and

The North Ridge, looking north from the Nick

Looking back at the traverse, from the Camp Four snowfield

Camp Four : Annapurna II behind

Annapurna I strange wispy tendrils reached up, breaking the light into its elemental colours before our eyes. Once more the world was at peace, and at last we could sit outside and enjoy it.

We knew where we wanted to go. Next morning found us beautifully placed on the glacier terrace between two large crevasses, those which had directed us towards the North Col and Snow Hump, about half an hour on from the first site. These crevasses would take anything the mountain cared to throw down, besides being a useful rubbish tip. Stores were dug out and transported in relays, tents erected, then we sat and waited for the returning Sherpas. They arrived at last, very tired from the heavy going, and flopped down with murmured thanks over their mugs of tea. The ice bulge above the Rognon had been bad, they said, and should have a fixed rope to it. Once again I reflected how easily we took this fine load-carrying of theirs, up and down remorselessly, for granted. Admittedly the sahibs on Machapuchare carried far more than I for one ever carried, but for two days, on Everest. And Charles always had an extra fifteen lbs or so of cine-equipment on top of his load. But that was partly because our proportion of Sherpas to sahibs was comparatively low. If we had been five to four all the time we might even have been in difficulties, for we had so much ironmongery, as well as over 2,000 feet of manila rope, in addition to the usual stores.

But the Sherpas reckon they are well paid for their labours, a fact easily forgotten. Apart from their daily wage, which this time included an unemployed period in Lehra, they receive at the end all their equipment, this being the established practice. We nearly caused a crisis at one stage by proposing not to give them their ice-axes. Poor Tashi, who already has five ice-axes at home, was made to lead a deputation from the Sherpas' Trades Union, and Jimmy had to give in. The real rub came when Dikshya Man, for doing exactly nothing, demanded exactly the same as the Sherpas.

So we lay and were grateful to Tashi and Ang Nyima and Ang Tsering. Apart from two loads at Camp One, to be fetched tomorrow, we were now fully supplied. We were in a position, if only the weather would amend its ways, to make a serious bid for the mountain.

CHAPTER SEVEN

A Big Effort

Forget men, everything
On this earth new-born,
Except that it is lovelier
Than any mysteries.
—EDWARD THOMAS

THE SAUSAGE showed again on 14th May. I noted it with disapproval, but not special concern. It had not always meant bad weather, and there had been about as much bad weather without it. Tashi and Ang Tsering set off down for Camp One, with one piton, a hundred feet of rope and a determination to safeguard the lower ice bulge, while Ang Nyima accompanied us upward to see how a Sherpa made out on the icy traverses. As we rose, we blessed Machapuchare's steepness for one thing: it very quickly sheds a coat of snow or hail, and much of what fell had already slithered in little snowballs down the couloirs. Our first Camp Two site was now obliterated. Great Gully always seemed a long pull-up; but at last it was done, and at last we had reached the bottom of the first fixed rope.

I had never before had the experience of climbing fixed ropes up a place previously climbed without. It is very agreeable. Gone the worry as to whether steps will hold, the forebodings at the green glint of ice. Easily and happily we swung upward, admiring the view, enjoying so much the final airy pull that we christened it Jacob's Ladder, since it clearly led to heaven. Blissful ourselves, we could not understand Ang Nyima's slowness. He came on doggedly, but seemed to disapprove. By 10.30 a.m. we were at the grotto, and Charles volunteered to go on with Ang Nyima, dumping a preliminary load of high-altitude rations and a tent, while David and I started to fix more ropes on the way down. This was a pleasant occupation, and by the end of that day 600 feet of good manila hung between Camps Two and Three.

Here let it be said that none of us considered himself an expert pitoneer in the modern sense. Before 1953 I had only struck one piton into rock, and that more in fear than anger, in the Central Gully of Lliwedd, North Wales. Indeed, with Menlove Edwards, I had removed two, from the Munich Climb on Tryfan, because we thought it so silly of these foreigners to need artificial aids. Times change. I have since struck one or two more into rock, still with an uneasy conscience, and with some pleasure into ice. The pegs that we drove into Machapuchare were for attaching a protective handrail, for belay and for bringing up Sherpas, not for overcoming steepnesses we could not otherwise have attempted. In that sense this was an ascent by the old school; though we did also use them later for getting down places which we could have climbed neither up nor down without.

Heavy nimbus had been brewing from the valley, and the snow started as we finished with the difficulties. Back in camp we lay listening to it, drinking tea and nibbling the good things which had been brought up: Vita-Weat with marmalade, cheese and nuts. From the Sherpas' tent came laughter, and some singing. In my diary I wrote: "When *will* it stop? It would be so nice to have tracks from one day to the next."

We had canvas overboots with us. As their name implies, these should go over the boot and add extra insulation, as well as keep out the snow. But Charles was the only one who could fit his on with crampons, and since he was an early riser these majestic objects were often the first thing visible when one looked out. On the 15th they were to be seen soon after 5 a.m. The morning was cold, with a strong wind. This shaded side of the ridge always meant miserably cold packing: climbing out and then in again, scraping snow off, pushing hard objects into ice-hardened sacks, burrowing for other objects in inches of new powder. Charles, in charge of stores, had worked out loads for two carries which would leave us with the necessities of life today and the luxuries to-morrow, if the Sherpas made two journeys. We were not off till 8 a.m., over snow which had well and truly buried the tracks of the day before. Bulging sacks made Jacob's Ladder rather less enjoyable this time, and the steps all had to be kicked out afresh. But by 12.30 we were up again, at a height which we at first reckoned optimistically to be 20,500 feet, but later, in more sober mood, just 20,000 feet. This time we were here to stay.

It was a memorable moment, but we were too thirsty to appreciate it. The little drink there was went to the Sherpas, who had come up well but slowly under Tashi's leadership. Besides his other beliefs, Tashi held firmly that sahibs cut steps too far apart, and his efforts to remedy this state of things had lost him three-quarters of an hour. The Sherpas started down to fetch the next lot; we levelled a platform, put up the tents and at long last lay brewing our lemon tea, drinking and talking, in that happy state of mind that altitude plus relaxation brings. We had put our sleeping-bags to dry over the tents, and it was in the middle of a sentence that I looked up, to see Charles's slither in a flash from his tent—and out of sight. It was the next crisis.

Charles, making tracks for the top of the *sérac*, was just in time to see it complete a magnificent 2,000-foot swoop and come to rest near the bottom crevasse, some 300 yards from Camp Two. There was one hope—at any rate for tomorrow. The time was 3.15 p.m. and the Sherpas, going cautiously, were only at the top of Great Gully. Charles shouted. They stopped, and seemed to be coming up. No, they went on down. He shouted again, we all shouted, and waved sleeping-bags. They *might* have understood.... Charles spent most of the remaining afternoon shouting on the *sérac*, but to no purpose. After four hours' descent we saw the three dots pass little more than a hundred yards from the bag. In the ensuing snow it was covered, and is lost for ever.

Charles accepted the challenge, without complaining. He spent the next nights wrapped in his and our down clothing, and even said that he slept well. Meanwhile, in the intervals of shouting, we admired the beauty of our position. Below us, nothing before the brown of the Base Camp moraine. To our right the immense line of flutings soared up in one alarming sweep, beyond which peeped the single jagged point of the Rock Gendarme. To the left the col, and above it a line of rising humps like shoulders covered in purest ermine. Beyond that the shapely giant, Annapurna III; and the eye which from there followed the great ridge ten miles westward, to Annapurna I, could not but pause in admiration at the sheer bulk of this tallest of the brothers, the broken line of its top and the snow sparkling over ochre rocks on its south-east face. Then the ridge dipped sharply south, to the rock spike called the Finger, and south again to the wavy crest of Ganesh. Down the valley a sea of cloud basked in silver light.

16th May. Again the excitement of a forward move, of a glimpse into the unknown. Perhaps it is because it paints all life's great moments in miniature that we fall for mountaineering. Camp Three however was another cold spot, and we did not get the right sensations until we were well started. The only way of escaping the site was to take a few steps left, into a steep little ice chimney which soon eased off on to the broad snow shelving of the upper face. This we reckoned would be amenable, by one or other of the gullies running up it, as far as the last 200 feet. The easiest line took us left again, then up a sizeable gully deep in snow. Near the top of this it was possible to chip steps out left, on to a steep snow-ice rib: a slow business, with always that airy crest tantalising against the blue above. Chip, chip, chip, step up. Chip, chip, chip, step up. About two hundred feet of it. And then, suddenly, I was there.

The view made me for a moment forget the others, forget everything. To the north the corniced crest sprang wildly away, over turret and pinnacle, to swing leftwards to the Snow Hump and North Col. Beyond the col, in an even fiercer series of giant ice leaves, vertically fluted, I could now see the ridge continue over minor summits, before it flattened finally against the broad bosom of Annapurna III. Looking south, all I could see was a steep pyramid of snow, our ridge being one of its edges: the so-called Rock Buttress, with not a speck of rock visible. And to the east, over the cloud-filled Seti, the smooth rocky head of Annapurna II peeped for the first time over the flattened shoulders of IV, giving the impression of a new and separate range.

We balanced gingerly on the corniced top. A few steps along our ridge, undertaken in the cause of cinematography, convinced me that there was no way there. But looking back I could see a little gully that descended almost directly under the crest on which the other two were uncomfortably perched. Also, looking down and

across to the far side of the Rock Buttress, we could just
see part of an innocent-looking little snowfield, about the
size of three football pitches. If these two, the gully and
the snowfield, could be connected, then we had got our
Camp Four. And this snowfield might well join up with
the level glacier whose existence we knew from Jimmy's
1950 photograph, a view very similar to that of the
Frontispiece.

An east face has the pleasant characteristic of receiving
early morning sunshine. But it is a doubtful benefit, since
sun on snow can also be disastrous. I started to cut away
the cornice, and realised that there was nothing below
but froth, the enormous suds of the giant's laundry.
Vigorous digging unearthed a patch hard enough to hold
a birch stake, which I hammered in, and on a hundred
feet of manila attached to this I was lowered into the void
beyond. The others safeguarded me on a climbing rope.
It was a horrible place; my first plunge landed me up to
the neck. Violent kicking got me farther down, relying
heavily on the manila round my wrist since rotten ice lay
under the snow. I had dropped my axe, but it jammed a
little way down. There followed a line of smooth rocks,
slightly overhanging and no help at all to the fumbling
feet. Now I was at the end of the rope, and at last on
reasonably solid snow.

The others followed, Charles without the protection of
a rope above. We tied on another hundred feet to get us
farther down the gully's continuation; but at the bottom
of that was nothing but a plunge to the glacier far below.

At this point we must leave the comfort of the rope and traverse horizontally, over whatever ribs and hollows separated us now from the snowfield. It was an un-pleasant crossing: ice-axe in, grasped firmly by both hands, kick twice and hope the step would stay. There was little danger of falling off, but a real one of falling into the slope, for the sun seemed to have loosened strange cavities below. The whole traverse of perhaps 400 yards took over an hour, its nastiest moment the crossing of another rock step. At half-past twelve, across a little guardian crevasse, we were at last resting and rejoicing on the first of the level snow.

It was such an ordinary little snowfield, I found myself expecting to see a talkative party of Frenchmen appearing from the col beyond, to hear some honest British language about the state of the snow. But all was silence. Biscuits, apricots, chocolate, then return. The traverse took only twenty-five minutes in the stamped-down steps. But we later decided, after discussion, that the pull up to 'the Nick', as we christened our cutting through the cornice on the ridge crest, seemed even more unpleasant than the descent from it. The feet were useless, the arms seemed to be pulling an immense and quite dead weight through sticky flour. Snow had started to fall from a greying sky, but we were stuffily warm still until we came out on to the ridge, where the prevailing west wind hit us. I fastened another hundred feet of rope to the birch stake on the west side, thus evening the burden, and started to skedaddle down that, chipping steps below as I went. The movement came awkwardly, since the lines of steps were diagonal, the rope never directly above and always faintly pulling sideways. More snow chased us down the couloir, and in our efforts to go fast we must have bunched up too close. A loud yell from David revealed that Charles had placed a heavily cramponed boot on his head. But the end was near. There now were the Sherpas, bearing in their hands that *sine qua non* of all returns—big mugs of 'hot sweet tea'. The crossing of the ridge could be done.

Depressing, this snow. I lay and listened to it with in-creased irritation each evening, and often to the thunder as well, picturing the good tracks covered over, the sacks and ropes that would have to be dug for. But the 17th was to be an off day, and it might clear, for we were still clinging pitifully to the fact that on Everest, in 1953, it had cleared from the middle of the month. We hoped a rest day would encourage the Sherpas for the 18th. Here Charles's knowledge of the language came in, as also his ability, given pencil and a bit of paper, to work out any logistics in a matter of minutes. The Sherpas were more worried by the difficulties of the Nick than by the fifty lbs. they would be carrying. We ourselves would be carrying forty lbs. or more, in the hope of being able to stay over the Nick for nearly a week if necessary. Some-how Charles managed to persuade Tashi and Ang Nyima (Ang Tsering would take it from his elders) that the sahibs would also make the way easy for them; and we devoted ourselves to the serious business of rest.

On an off day, unfortunately, there are always jobs crying to be done, those jobs which you uneasily remember having "put off till we have a day in camp". One of these was the taking of the photographs which are modern advertisement's incursion into the field of mountaineering. Firms had asked for them, in return for gifts of food, and David was therefore photographed handing a brand of biscuit to me, while I looked up at it in what was supposed to be greedy anticipation. Tashi poured soup into a pan, over an efficient-looking Primus. And so on. Then Charles did some filming as we secured the ice chimney above camp with a length of manila. Then the afternoon snow and thunder set in, and we retired like Israel in dudgeon to our tents.

At 5 a.m. on the 18th the snow lay so thick that we debated leaving it another day. Then we pulled ourselves together and got the porridge going. The Sherpas looked dubiously at the snow and were slow climbing out, so we started taking down two of the tents, leaving a third standing in reserve. At 8.25 we were away, digging out the rope in the ice chimney, furrowing our deep track up the gully. At the rope end I drove in a piton and unfurled another 100-foot length. The whole of the steeper section was now protected, and the Sherpas kept close on our heels, enjoying it.

At the top Tashi swung off his heavy load, very cautiously because there was little room, and peered dubiously through the hole in the cornice the other side. But he said nothing. We divided forces. I dived through the Nick, in what was supposed to be a neat demonstration of how it should be done. It was not very convincing. After 100 feet I stopped, exhausted, and David came on; then the three Sherpas, protected by Charles up on the windy ridge. His position, however, seemed little less enviable than ours, for the heat on this sunward side was intense, and there was no room to take off clothes. To cool us down, chips and splinters of ice came showering painfully from above.

Tashi wriggled awkwardly through the hole, his great sack looking from below far bulkier than himself. He started to lower but tried, as I thought he would, to cut steps. This proved quite hopeless; for one thing he found it impossible to hang on with one arm alone. He continued grimly, silently. When it was his turn Ang Tsering slid with agility down the first and steepest section. But just above the rocks he slipped, and his weight came on the climbing rope. He had the presence of mind to keep his hold on the fixed rope and hung there, quite calmly against the snow, until David could scramble up and put his feet in steps that did just exist if you looked for them. Sucking sweets he and I, with Tashi, started off to remake the traverse. Quite unmoved by his slip, Ang Tsering balanced with the ease of a young gymnast across the intricacies of hollow snow, and even the rock. This was the only patch of rock on which we trod after the Rognon, and like most rock patches it was no help at all. The angle of it pushed you out, the snow needed to be scraped off, and the steps into the safety beyond had to be carefully timed. By the time we reached the snowfield the traditional afternoon fall had set in, and we tramped through it to a spot noted beforehand: just short of a little level ridge about thirty feet high that bounded our snowfield, barred our way and ended in an innocent-looking snow bump, easy to contour. During the tent pitching I stood back for a minute and could not help smiling at the scene of determined misery. As fast as everything was set down, snow buried it. Figures unrecognisable in their blue hoods pulled at strings, pulled things out of sacks, bumped into each other, stamped down pegs, warmed hands in pockets, started all over again. Somehow the tents were up, the longed-for moment had arrived: squashed in wet sleeping-bags we were lying side by side trying to eat sardines.

After an hour or so the patter eased, the mist drew apart. Charles, indefatigably out for a walk, summoned us to "come and see". The mountain's beauty was hard to believe. Dimmer than in Plate 17, but with the same evening sun lighting up the loveliness of its ice flutings, the summit cone seemed to peer over at us like a great beast, watching. Out of the white mist it rose, above the intervening little ridge, to dominate our world. Once again, looking at it, I stopped wondering how we would get up, or even whether we would get up at all. Camp Five, yes, somewhere near the shoulder shelf hunched below those last steep thousand feet. But for the moment it was enough just to admire it, to reverence it even. Charles stamped up to the snow shoulder and returned thoughtful. It might not be so easy to get on to the upper glacier after all, he said. But there would be a way, as there had been before. For the moment it seemed more important that we had left the milk powder behind, and had to have supper without it.

* * *

Three in a two-man tent is a crowd, but for Charles in his down suiting warmer than a tent of one's own. It was a long business getting everything on, and he ended looking like a Michelin man. Next morning we profited from the much maligned sun, for it was warm and pleasant packing and we set off for Camp Five in high spirits, with big loads, soon after 7 a.m. The snow shoulder was only ten minutes' tramp away, across level snow. For practical purposes that was as far as we got that day.

"Ghastly" I wrote in my diary of the view, in very different mood from the evening before. At the level shoulder, just left of the little bump, we stopped, perforce. Instead of leading straight to the upper glacier, clearly visible to the right in its great sweep up to the summit steepness, our snowfield just came to an end, like that. We looked down. Thousands of feet below, as it seemed, a valley was filling with mist. Above it and to the right we could see the huge blocks into which the upper glacier broke, but to see them more clearly we must climb the little bump and this, seen end-on, did not look at all as innocent as before.

The bump was really the end of a subsidiary ridge descending at right-angles from the Rock Buttress, which on this side had given up all pretence of being rock and flaunted a skyline of defiant ice pinnacles. The bump, only some forty feet high, stopped me on its top with unexpected sharpness. David came up, I started to traverse the hundred feet or so separating us from the main buttress. (To avoid this traverse we later put the rope ladder, visible in Plate 17. The bump is also visible, to its left.) It was absurd, ridiculous. Twenty-five feet down on my right a little bergschrund guarded the gentle névé on which the one remaining tent of Camp Four sat sunning itself, only 200 yards away. But the immediate crest was as sharp as any I had been on, and the view down to the left alarming. For the great upper glacier did indeed break off, but inconsiderately just short of, and lower than, our position. It broke into chunks and slices that gradually, as they descended, lost all semblance of glacier orderliness and tumbled into titanic chaos. On its right (true left) side the glacier did extend towards us, some 300 feet below our level, a thin shelf of fairly level snow. To reach this, as we had reached Camp Four by the traverse, was what we must now try to do.

David and I spent the next three hours and more trying to do it, having first got rid of our loads by rolling them down on to the flats to the right. We tried traversing: but the snow was far steeper than on the earlier traverse, and even more rotten in that it was inlaid with blocks of ice, ready to slide away with the mush on top. I made a

Machapuchare summit from near Camp Four. (The little ice ride and the fixing of the rope ladder are visible on the right, Rock Gendarme behind)

The ice ridge above Camp Four

few steps, then retreated, seldom having felt less secure. Charles, who had been filming our antics, tried with the Sherpas to make a more direct way up over the schrund; but without success, for at that point the little ridge bulged out like an onion, and was thicker above the schrund than at its level. Then we tried to reach the main obstructing ridge at a higher point, in the hope of better ground. The last few feet up proved all but impossible, not from any technical difficulty but from the bottomless mass of snow which did no more than hold in support the one or two ice blocks composing the crest. When we finally peered over, the traverse looked even steeper than before. We went down.

The realists of the party had re-erected the second tent, and at midday, when we should have been nearing a splendid camp site on the high shoulder below the final steepness, at 22,000 feet, we lay disconsolately at only 20,400, pondering this penultimate obstacle which looked like defeating us altogether. What to do now? Have a light party imitating Hermann Buhl on Nanga Parbat and trying for the summit from here, in the cold of night? Go round and approach by the Seti? It was David who said, reflectively:

"If we had four hundred feet of rope we might lower ourselves and just hit that glacier shelf."

It had not occurred to us to give up. The mountain had shown so many improbabilities to be possible after all, opening so many cunning back doors to the patient. If we had hit the north ridge a hundred yards to the right,

or to the left, we could probably never have got down.
If there had been no exit from Gardyloo. . . . Might we
not be lucky again? We decided that we might, if we
went right back to Base and brought up all available rope
and a rope ladder to obviate the little ridge. Then we lay
waiting for a chance to go back to the ridge and have
another look, just to make sure.

But the afternoon snow persisted till 8 p.m. and the
20th dawned without its usual brilliance. Another
sausage, formed over Annapurna II, barred the early rays,
and we wondered how Charles Evans and Dennis Davies
were faring in their attempt on that bald rock crown.
Before starting down, we went up once more to the near
snow shoulder. Charles and David anchored firmly and
let me lower myself on all the available rope, 220 feet,
straight down. The view was not good, for this side of
the ridge consisted of ribs and furrows in the old style.
However, by working over to the nearest rib I got a
glimpse of the shelf extending towards and below me
like the finger of a hand, the other fingers having been
broken off in the gigantic ruin on its left. To my estimat-
ing eye the drop from the ridge above would be less than
400 feet. If our rope allowed us to reach the shelf, we
could walk up it easily and on to the broad upper glacier.
Then, for practice, I climbed back up the rope on my
hands, my legs arched against the loosening slope.

The Sherpas had packed up all that we needed to take
back to Base, and at 8.40 we started. This time, perhaps
because there had been little sun, the surface below the

Nick was harder. I left Tashi, my second, and wound the fixed rope round my right wrist, cutting with the left hand. The surface was still too soft to take a piton, and far too steep to allow me to stand in balance. It proved the most strenuous half-hour of the expedition, and the next hour and a quarter, waiting in the wind on top for the others to join me, about the coldest. Ang Tsering, coming up, tangled his rope with the fixed rope. . . . At last we were down the fixed ropes on the other side, and in the warmth of Camp Three.

On 21st May we were to be at Base, but my sense of eager haste was irritated by the need for more step-cutting down the top of Great Gully. On the plain of Camp Two we stopped to search, in vain, for Charles's sleeping-bag. It was a hard struggle between virtue and sloth, and we soon gave up. At the camp itself we stopped much longer, to rest and eat and admire Tashi's energy as he dug out tents and brought stores along to Charles for inventory. Then on, past Camp One and into the gutter of Gardyloo, which had lost much of its earlier romance in two weeks of rubbish dumping. The ice-curtains were crumbling into drab ruin, stones and grass tufts littered the dirty snow-bed. At the bottom, however, to our great content, clear water flowed, birds sang, brown grass looked as if it would some day be green. As we neared Ang Nyima's bridge a figure in a red sweater could be seen sitting on a rock: Jimmy, who had returned from Pokhara and come down to ease the burden of that last and most laborious climb.

CHAPTER EIGHT

A Hundred and Fifty
Feet to go

Who aimeth at the sky
Shoots higher much than he who meant a tree.
—George Herbert

"Jamais nous ne goûtons de parfaite allégresse." So said one
of Corneille's characters, in a moment of chagrin, and I
applauded his sentiments during our three days at Base.
For Base Camp should be a place of pure delight, of
streams and grass and birds, of easy lying and good eating.
The latter is important, but a man with toothache, or a
gumboil as mine turned out to be, cannot even enjoy the
former. Those three days of rest were not as happy as
they were designed to be; only on the third evening I
succeeded in squeezing the poison out with cotton wool
and finding peace.

Jimmy told of the journey down with Roger. They
had done it in five days, splendid going when they had
had to hack out a broader path through the bamboo.
Three coolies had carried him in turn, but as he was

facing backwards, his head had been in constant danger. Near Kuldighar they had been met by Miss Steel and Dr. Turner, who had come up in record time and now examined him. They approved, it seemed, the treatment or lack of it that he had been having, then sped back to their patients as quickly as they had come. The journey continued, and must have been as tiring for the coolies as for Roger and Jimmy, whose big responsibility it was. Back at Pokhara and in good hands, Roger was having to spend a month in quarantine. Jimmy said that our misfortune had got mixed up in some papers with an accident to the Yorkshire Ramblers' party, elsewhere in Nepal. This might worry our families, and therefore worried us; for the mail had not been getting through as well as we had hoped.

We owed a lot to the lonely British hospital of Pok-hara. Back in England Roger, who is a determined person, very soon took to crutches, then to two sticks, then to one. By October he was doing a severe rock climb in North Wales, though he still uses his stick on the level. He has time ahead, to come back to Nepal.

Jimmy was accompanied back by an engaging but very stupid character known as 'Moti' (fat one). He was to be our mail runner, with disastrous results to any moneys entrusted to him. On the way up Moti had spotted a *jharal* on the cliffs above the Modi gorge. Loads were dropped, the Tally-ho went up and some desperate rock climbing followed, waistbands coming in useful as rope. At one point Moti had got hold of the *jharal's* leg, but it had shaken free. Finally, and this must be very unusual, it was persuaded to fall off its ledge and was dispatched with Jimmy's ice-axe. Even after removal of the entrails it took five men (Moti on all fours underneath) to carry it back to Hinko. The carcass had been divided and brought up, in tasty joints.

Moti had the keen eyes of a hillman. He could point out a group of *jharal* grazing far away among cliff greenery, for which we needed binoculars. It was only a pity that there was nothing much behind those eyes that looked so sage.

On the 23rd a newspaper article and letters must be written. Ang Nyima, Da Temba and Ang Tsering spent much of the time playing a kind of dice game, in which the dice were shaken from a meat tin and points scored according to a system which I never managed to fathom. We sometimes wondered whether Ang Tsering's chants on the mountain were a *miserere* for his misspent gambling youth, or a prayer to the gods to avert the day's dangers. We talked to them about the yeti, or Abominable Snowman, the still legendary figure of the snows who at the time of writing is about to become the prey of a full-scale American expedition. All of the Sherpas lived in what might be called the heart of the Snowman country, but none of them had seen, or even knew anyone who had seen, a *yeti*. Ang Nyima seemed to think it very unlikely that he would be caught.

Tashi, meanwhile, had more serious work in hand. He was constructing a twenty-five foot rope ladder. This was a cunning contrivance of split birch threaded in manila rope, and it weighed only six pounds. We tested it on a boulder, with Dikshya Man as sheet anchor, and it gave great satisfaction. Poor Dikshya Man had had a boring time, and had finished *Hope for the Troubled*. He now started on my copy of Orwell's *Nineteen Eighty-Four*, and the slogans like "War is Peace" and "Freedom is Slavery" seemed to him excellent. That afternoon he sat in on our plans, while a heavy storm of thunder and hail recalled early days.

We reckoned, on a computation of loads by Charles, that two sahibs and one Sherpa could sleep at Camp Five, with food for two days; one sahib would escort two more Sherpas back, and a third stay in support on the west side of the Nick. In my diary I jotted down "factors for success" in these terms: (a) ability to get safely down on to the upper glacier; (b) a high top camp; (c) a support party which could have a second shot; (d) the summit pyramid not being as bad as it looks. In the event only factor (a) operated, and that partially, since only two could get down. On the other hand the Goddess of the mountain, on whom we had not counted, intervened to take a kindly interest.

The last attempt began on 24th May. Jimmy, who felt he had lost acclimatisation, started for Camp One, and then Two, with Tashi, so that he could spend an extra day up there and also take important survey photographs. Dhanbahadur and Da Temba carried extra food to Camp One, and returned. For the rest it was a day of peace, and a quiet evening with only some high mackerel cirrus to sound a warning note. I wandered up the ablation valley, admiring its running water and grass, its potentillas and primulas and dwarf anemones, its redstarts flitting over the stream. I sat down to look at our peak, and started this poem:

A monster torn out of the womb of ages,
a rock-bound sheath folding a blade of snow,
a cloud bent over, a mass hoisted from ocean,
a man's thought homing to God from pain below—

whichever of these, your wide horns are above me.
I have now fought you, and now wondering sit
why I so wrestled, or so prayed to bestride you,
your cold, hard body, and where was the use of it.

Mosses and primula soothe, where I am sitting.
Swallow and redstart flit on the tumbling stream.
These call me to calm in the Abiding,
In the sacred thought, not in the ambitious dream.

I only know that tomorrow I shall be stepping
up the patterned ridge, to the rockhead mountain crown;
as if it mattered, that one hour to be standing
on a crested wave of the world—and then come down.

But it was not to be tomorrow, for Da Temba—prosaic anticlimax—had gone up without goggles and by

Near the bottom of the 'cut-off'. (The fixed rope is just visible in the ice gully behind)

Looking down on Rock Buttress (at last). Above Camp Five

Looking back at the ice ridge, cut-off and shelf from upper glacier

evening lay in an agony of snow-blindness, unable to move. The 25th dawned grey and dull, and after debate we decided to leave Jimmy another day on his own and go up in force on the 26th. Charles, David and I explored the rock shoulder of Hiunchuli immediately above camp: an excursion notable for a 2,000-foot glissade and a reasonably close view of a *jharal* making its stately way off the snow into the brown camouflage of adjoining hillside. Charles, athirst to film it, was brought up dead by an impossible rock face over which it had seemed to wander with ease.

26th May. Candles, matches, Profol for stoves, tobacco, books, cutlery—all the little things packed at last, and away on as unpromising a morning as an expedition can ever have chosen. Dikshya Man came 300 yards down with us and wrung our hands. "Bless and God save you! I must go now." He rushed back to camp, as if for an important appointment. Grey storm cloud filled the valleys, Gardyloo was dirty with scraggy grass tufts perched on snow that would have disgraced a London street. The exit was now sordid ice, needing steps. At 11 a.m. snow started to fall, more like rain than snow, and Camp One leaked badly. We spread a plastic sheet over the worst patch. I could cheerfully have given the whole expedition up there and then. But the 27th dawned cloudless, the air was crisp again; in better heart we struggled with heavy sacks to the Rognon, then on, up to our knees, towards the higher terrace. As we rested there at last, after three hours' going, little snowballs, growing larger in the warm sun, started rolling out of the gullies above, slowing down on gentler ground. Suddenly one phalanx of them seemed larger and faster than it should be. I wriggled myself to one side, David slithered a few feet, Charles, in the direct line, was carried some thirty feet down and lay there, looking comically up, his goggles awry over his face. He scrambled out to rescue his load, undamaged but complaining, and David went back to see if the Sherpas, out of sight on the steeper rise below, were all right. We continued with the track and were met by Jimmy and Tashi coming out from Camp Two. David said, afterwards, that at first he had been shaken to see only the loads, upright in the furrowed snow. The Sherpas had abandoned them and fled to a protecting eave of ice. A disconcerting experience for all, and proof that odd things can happen, even in the mildest places. The Sherpas arrived, palpably upset and not realising that in fact they had been in no serious danger, to be soothed by tea and rest from the broiling sun.

Our whole active force was now at Camp Two. One load remained at One, to be collected next day by Ang Tsering and Da Temba. And Jimmy, pursuing the beau-ideal of the surveying scientist, had at last taken his necessary angles and photographs. He wanted to make his own first visit to Three, and did this on the 28th with Tashi and Ang Nyima, taking up a first instalment of loads. Charles, David and I found odd jobs around camp in preparation, and made the inevitable computations. It was beginning to look as if, to get two men to the top, we should aim at not more than six over the Nick, with thirty days' food (five days' for each man). That would mean safety, and support from the remaining two behind. Moreover Da Temba, a nervous little man, might not make the Nick anyway. Charles licked his pencil and got to work again in earnest.

The others had a long day and did not get down till after 5 p.m. having reached the grotto. Tashi had been magnificent, Jimmy said, leading nearly all the way as he knew it best. In places there had been eighteen inches of new snow to clear. We put the problems; and Jimmy generously suggested that he should do the carrying to Three, with Da Temba and the supporting party, then return to Base to continue his survey. It must have been as hard a decision as his earlier one, over Roger, from which it stemmed. The mountain was his, the original plan and the idea of getting over the north ridge to the snowfields beyond. But the decision made sense.

That evening was a fine one, full of hope. A delicate salmon-pink tipped the black mass of cumulus down the valley, just for a few moments before evening's grey hands went racing up the peaks. There was welcome cold in the air, and even the summit peered in a less forbidding way than usual over that long intervening ridge.

The decision seemed still more sensible the next morning. For this blessed once we were using the tracks of a previous day's party, and luxury they seemed. The leading rope, moving with joyful speed, did not realise what was happening at the rear. Da Temba, it turned out, had taken one look at the steep section and said he felt giddy. Jimmy decided wisely to take him straight down, from there. This we learned later, after reaching camp in record time, from the other three. All of them used what Charles described as picturesque language about the faint-heartedness of Darjeeling Sherpas, for only poor Da Temba was not a stalwart Sola Khumbu man.

It was here that the idea of collapsing tents during absence came in for the worst abuse. For several days the sun had shone, the snow had fallen. Alternately it had frozen and thawed, frozen and thawed, and frozen again. The surface of the tents held two puddles of ice firmly embedded in the material. Every square inch of canvas must be chipped away; and it was impossible, at times, for the chipping axe to avoid tearing through below. The Edgington suffered many small rents and one major gash. After nearly two hours, when one tent was up, Ang Nyima and Ang Tsering made themselves a drink and went down for the abandoned load. Their voices, still raised querulously against Darjeeling Sherpas, disappeared over the edge. Tashi pulled out his needle and prepared to stitch the gash. That afternoon it was fine, after a token storm on the way up, and our grouses disappeared one by one. Charles filmed a bout of specially laid-on step-cutting in the chimney above; and the day ended in the calm of a glowing sunset over the Ganesh ridge.

30th May also stayed reasonably fine, and we set Camp Four on its feet, this time with almost a week's food and limitless rope. In an evening of clearing skies David and

I climbed along the little ridge, finding it easier this time to take it *à cheval*, and fixed the famous rope ladder. (The operation shown in Plate 17.) This time we used a spare ice-axe as belay, and on the side of the upper glacier started gaily throwing down our spare rope attached to it. But it became obvious that throwing straight down would get us only straight to the Seti. We would have to work right, over a crumbling rib of snow, to get a view of our glacier shelf which lay just out of sight below. At that we left it, for the day. Descending the rope ladder gave a feeling of luxury after the gymnastics of the ridge; but of all the day my clearest impression is the sense of somebody watching, behind. The great beast with which I had identified the summit wedge, its striped face shot with the last sun, its body hunched on icy haunches, was peering over the little ridge at us, not spitefully or even amusedly, but in a strangely remote and impersonal way, as if it were watching, just watching.

The 'rope trick' was going to take longer than we had reckoned, and the 31st therefore was given up to the major operation. For all (except the Sherpas) it was a bad night, not just because we were three in the tent and each felt the repercussions when the others turned, but we had omitted to drink much the day before, our throats were dry and in the morning we sat gulping tea weakly in the sun, dreading a move. At 7.30, having no further excuse, we plodded up carrying our spare coils. Arrived at the ridge, I plucked a spare ice-axe from the snow—and a 220-foot length of Roger's nylon, looped round, went slithering down into nothing. No place, this, to compromise with folly. Enough was left, however, for me to grasp two 100-foot lengths knotted together and start sliding down, protected by the others. First I must work over to the rib. This, when reached, resembled a bank of feathers, giving no hold. For some minutes I stamped about; at last it was possible to wedge in another spare ice-axe for extra belay, and start down the ice gully on the far side. This was the crux: a narrow couloir of over seventy degrees in places, partly sheltered and therefore partly ice, but bad ice. I cut steps where I could, relied wholly on the rope where I could not, slithered gratingly down and tried not to lose my axe. Near the rope's end, under an evil bulge, a fragment of embedded rock could be cleared so that one could just stand, uncomfortably, on its top rim. I extracted a last length of manila and tied that on; to my joy, by flicking it glacierward again, I could just make it reach a point separated by only thirty feet or so of apparently easy ground from the glacier shelf, here at its terminus a bank of slanting snow. Above, the others could not hear me. I started climbing back up the rope, chiefly on my hands.

We reached camp again at about 9.30 a.m. It must have been the heat, and the effects of a bad night, that made us lie panting like tired dogs for the rest of the day, drinking immoderately. As the sun climbed higher my limbs felt more and more leaden, the possibility of getting anywhere tomorrow more and more remote. Tomorrow! We should be packing things now, making a plan! Far better to turn over and go to sleep again—but when I turned, the heat pricked, sweat started out uncomfortably in my vest. I would move restlessly, trying an easier position. We *must* make plans.

It is a truism that yesterday's difficulties become the easy walks of tomorrow. Ang Nyima and Ang Tsering had doubted whether they could get over the Nick at all. Now, they volunteered to return across it alone, leaving the four of us at Camp Four with more food, more room and a potential support from Three. We in our camp lay considering the next days. We could not reasonably invite Tashi down the 'cut-off', as it was dubbed, nor did he volunteer. I thought he would be safe alone at Four, but Charles, with logistics in mind, reckoned that two was a safer number for the support party, and volunteered to stay too, leaving to David and me the distinct honour but dubious pleasure of carrying Camp Five as high as we could. So it was settled; I knew Charles had wanted to film the top, and feared that there might be a depth of self-sacrifice behind his generosity. But we also felt that he preferred to be taken at his word.

Primuses started early, at 4 a.m., on the glorious First of June. The two loads were inevitably heavy, since besides a tent, sleeping-bags, Li-Los, stove and cine camera (the mantle had fallen on David), we had food for three days, 500 feet of nylon line and one or two pitons. These loads we hoisted up the rope ladder, but we could not avoid donning them on the beaten platform of the little ridge. By 6.30 a.m. I was launching away,

protected by climbing rope. Familiarity with the place
was offset by the load on my back, and I was breathless,
infuriated and dishevelled by the time I came to rest on
the embedded rock. I sent up the climbing rope. Half
an hour followed, and no movement from above. At
first it was pleasant to stand there admiring the hugeness
of the tumbled glacier blocks below, to estimate the
distance to the sunny shelf of glacier. Then I started to
worry. The snow would be softening, our glacier tramp
heating up. Besides, I was very cramped. . . .

We had left our ropes hanging the day before. When
David appeared, encumbered by his heavy load and particularly the marker flags sticking out from the top, he
said that another climbing rope had frozen into the ridge,
and that they had been trying to free it. Coming down
for the first time laden, he could not see such knobs as
there were and reached me in an even worse state than my
own. We were now cut off from Charles but attached
by our own climbing rope, which we belayed to a piton
hammered in just above the embedded rock. I swarmed
down over a second little rib and was startled to find the
'gentle' ground not to be snow at all, but brittle ice on
rock, with only an inch or two of overlay. We were now
descending diagonally from the piton, and would not
have enough fixed rope to take us all the way. I cut off
twenty feet of climbing rope, shortening the length
between us to eighty feet. With the help of this I just
reached the shelf. David, who had had to come lower to
secure me, descended the last few holdless feet, his boots

Approaching the final steepness : snow above the knees

The highest picture : on the lower part of the final face

skidding. He was swearing audibly. (Plate 19; the rope down the gully is just visible behind.) But we had arrived.

We had taken two whole hours down, and the shelf was steeper than had seemed. Still, we had arrived, and it remained only to toil along it until it joined the parent glacier. The sun was now well above, our movements slow. Soon we were resting, and drinking the little we had brought. We went on. Every half-hour, then every twenty minutes, we changed the lead. Looking back (Plate 20a) we could see Charles on the little ridge. We could also see what a freak of mountain architecture was our shelf, for it seemed quite simply to be plastered to the mountain-side, ready one day to go crashing down among the fragments.

Anxiety kept us on the move, for we knew that two crevasses still barred the way. The first proved a giant which spanned the whole width of the upper glacier: it gave no alternative but to go left, alongside its great overhanging jaws, until it petered out among the mighty blocks bounding us on that side. We dragged ourselves wearily over, then steered back again towards the centre. "It must be glacier lassitude," we said, at the welcome stopping-places. But it was exciting to see ourselves at last passing the Rock Buttress, at last coming under the curious line of ice spires which connect it, on this side, with the Rock Gendarme. Then the second crevasse appeared, cavernous and hopeless. We moved despondently along it; and there, suddenly, a delicate ice bridge greeted us, as if it had been put out for our especial benefit, that very moment.

We plodded very little farther, then camped gratefully on the flat above. Mist was already moving purposefully about, and if we started early tomorrow, we said, we could move more quickly, without loads, up snow hardened in the night. The height must have been about 21,000 feet, the time was 12.30 p.m. At first the sun shone and we sat outside the tent admiring the great beast that still seemed to peer down at us above its hunched shoulder. Then the mist turned to a light snow, the great whiteness above disappeared. We lay talking, missing the distraction of our books, and listening. It did not stop till after 7 p.m. and still the night seemed warm.

An early start without alarm clock always makes me wake every hour, and I woke finally at 2 a.m. wondering whether to suggest starting already. At 2.45 we lit the Primus. To simplify cooking we would eat Grape-Nuts, and needed only to heat water for milk and tea. I remember a long discussion, in the unreal candlelight, as to whether we might not get some money from the makers, if we said that we had chosen Grape-Nuts only for our summit breakfast. Would the advertisement be thought good enough? We could not decide. Outside it was still very dark and quiet, and much colder. A pale cloud hung over Annapurna II, our own summit blotted out the stars. The weather looked good. We started putting on crampons at 3.45 a.m. but we had underestimated the cold and dark. We tried the candle outside—it blew out.

It took over twenty minutes for freezing, fumbling fingers to adjust the straps. At 4.20 we finally stepped out.

To my dismay the snow, even here, came over the ankles. It had not had time to pack down. Even so, the tramp up the easy glacier remains in memory a vivid delight. We had had few such spells, with no immediate worry ahead. For this short time we seemed to be triumphing, at last, over all the obstacles. Only smooth snow lay before us to be tramped; and meanwhile much that had seemed impossible lay below, for us to look down upon it as the gods must look. To the north a host of unnamed peaks showed grey in the distance beyond the shoulder of Annapurna IV. Slowly, as we looked back, the impostor of a Rock Buttress began to sink, and at last we came abreast of the Rock Gendarme itself. We turned left, up steeper snow leading to Machapuchare's final shoulder, and began to top even the Gendarme. Beyond it and far below we could see the brown moraine against which Base Camp nestled, and above that, far away beyond the Finger, the peaks of the Dhaulagiri Himal.

"If the weather holds we might do it," I said, and we could both feel the excitement, without needing to say more.

But the snow was now almost to our knees, and every twenty minutes the lead changed. We came slowly on to the great sloping shoulder, the site once proposed for our top camp. There we stopped at 7 a.m. for food, and reckoned that we had less than a thousand feet to go.

Those feet lay back a little more amenably in their general angle than had seemed before, it is true, but they now revealed themselves to be made up of glittering ribs of pure blue ice. The only hope, if we had no more than the day to play with, lay on the snow wedged in runnels between the lines of fluting. It looked best to keep rather left, then to cross right, up a line of weakness under the startlingly jagged left-hand skyline, near the top. We started for the little bergschrund under the face.

In the next four hours time seemed to stand still, and very little to be happening. Yet we were moving almost continuously, and not seeming to feel the height. David, leading the last stretch to the schrund, went in over his knees. Above it I cut a line of steps to the right, then left, until we could get on to the first snow that would support us. We rose very slowly. The half-hours passed and still we struggled, on snow or ice. It seemed a long time before we passed above the great triangular overhang which is a feature of the right-hand skyline; still longer before 'the Onion', a mighty globe of ice the size of a cottage on the left-hand ridge, sank below. Indeed this onion seemed to hold us fascinated for hours, both by its size and by its position on the very ridge-crest. The act of getting above it seemed a major triumph in itself. Behind us, but we had no time to admire them, all the peaks, from Manaslu over the Annapurna range to Dhaulagiri, basked in an almost saffron light. And then, suddenly, it was not so.

When we looked up at about 9 a.m. it was to see a line

of mackerel cloudlets hurrying from the west. In a matter of minutes each peak had donned a dull, ominous coif of 'sausage' cloud. Out of a sky still bright with sun behind, the snow started to fall. At first softly, then faster, and the sun hid himself behind the dun curtains.

We tried to hurry, but it seemed to make no difference. Besides, the going was not easy. Two ice chimneys led right, above the Onion and under the crest of the ridge, steep and awkward and filled with doubtful snow. For this snow on the chimney walls was crumbling already, with ice blocks pushing through like young turnips in a turnip field. The bouts of step-cutting became more frequent. Just before 11 a.m. I rounded a rib, very near the top of everything as I thought, and saw four or five columns of blue ice, like the claws of some great dragon, thrusting up each to its place on the summit ridge: it was the summit itself, perhaps a little under 150 feet above our heads. The claws were swept and dusted of snow. David came up, I hacked two more steps. Each took many blows. It looked as if the Goddess had drawn her firm line here, at least for these her two respectably married suitors. With that we must be content.

If it had not been snowing so hard, we could have eaten and considered what might have been, in good conditions, a two- or three-hour job. As it was, we made our decision almost without speaking, and David turned imperturbably to the important ritual of lighting a pipe. This, in the snow that fell faster and faster, proved even more profitless than my task of unfurling 500 feet of nylon line. Making a mistake which no Second-Class Boy Scout should make, I had left them as the maker packs them in my sack. At last, with some losses, they were out, and attached to a most welcome piton. Even with this handrail the steep upper face pushed us awkwardly out; the ice chimneys, now masked with powder, allowed no certainty to the next step. We swarmed into them, clutching their sides, and straddled out. Soon we were peering as anxiously for the polished globe of the Onion below as we had previously sought to overtop it. And we were glad, when its roundness showed indistinct through the grey. The snow runnels below had forgotten our steps; and when we came to the lowest ice they were only just to be seen, picked out in white relief. That stage was very tiresome, chiefly because our bodies must twist to fit the angle of the ice, to spy the line below. I went first, chipping out fresh steps between the relics of our early morning enthusiasm. My back ached with the effort of bending, my eyes were confused with the probing flakes. David, behind, suffered both from the awkwardness of steps I had skimped and the responsibility of last man. The shoulder, when it came, seemed broad as the Atlantic Ocean and welcoming with the promise of knee-deep tracks. We started down it with relief.

The relief did not last long. The tracks, although knee-deep, had drifted over and soon disappeared completely. We had a compass, and had left one marker flag. For the rest, it was a miserable journey, in mist so white that we almost fell, unable to distinguish between air and earth; in murk so thick that only the next few yards could be seen at all. Gone the conquering zest of early morning, when each gigantic feature of the mountain had seemed to acknowledge our victory. Now we were very small, very humble and rather wet. I had pushed back the hood of my windproof, to be able to see on either side. Soon beard and forelock were a mess of caked snow and dripping icicles. The flat glacier stretched endlessly. . . . Surely we had missed the tent? Surely those great hummocks on the left belonged to some different mountain altogether? There were no gullies like this that we were following on Machapuchare. We *must* be wrong. . . . No, the square black rectangle of the little tent welcomed us in the half-light. At 2.30 p.m. we were pulling off crampons and crawling with shivers into the longed-for dryness of down.

As I lay thinking back over the day I could not feel a real disappointment not to have stood upon the crest itself, those few feet above. Irritation, perhaps, at not knowing whether we could be said to have climbed the mountain—but after all that was a matter for individual judgment, and provided our own was satisfied. . . . More than anything we must be grateful, to have been allowed up so many improbabilities and by so narrow a chain of chance; to have been stopped, so positively and so near, not having to gamble our safety on the gods' further pleasure. No, we were very lucky.

That night I did not sleep well. David had prudently

taken a sleeping-pill, and I had his aggravatingly peaceful breathing in my ear. Partly it may have been that my hair had never really dried, and I would shiver occasionally. Perhaps owing to snow, perhaps to earlier effort, I did not seem able to control my nose or mouth very well, and would wake with a sticky dribble down one side of my face. The meat bar hoosh that night, though a good one, had seemed unappetising and I had stuck to soup: perhaps we had been on the things too long. And then I was thinking, thinking and dreaming back over the day. In a year or two I would almost have forgotten it, and that would be a pity. If only I could live slower, to savour each minute of friendship and effort, of hope and relief! At last I slept.

The 3rd chased us down with a ring round the sun and the promise of more snow. We had not even time to photograph the tent, but packed it hastily. On the way up it had swayed and danced irritatingly on top of David's sack; this time, with determination, we managed to squeeze it in. Then we wasted minutes looking for the cine equipment, which I was to carry. It was only when we reached Four that we found it had been packed in the tent. Going down the glacier was a very different business from coming up. I took many photographs (unfortunately omitting to remove an orange filter which gave to colour shots a bright orange hue). At last we were on the shelf. We were shouting to Charles, some 350 feet above. The dreaded 'cut-off' took as long to climb up as to descend, the thirstiest two hours I remember. During the first part we could not be protected by the climbing rope, as everything had frozen in. But at the top sat Charles, not *on* the ridge but twenty-five feet *below* it, in a tunnel that he and Tashi had carved out at its thinnest part. It was good to take the stràin off arms and legs; to grasp hands and to be ministered to, back at camp, with mugs of tea by Tashi; to talk and listen, and to hear the snow beating out its fury above our heads.

CHAPTER NINE

Savoury to a Fish Tail:
Fluted Peak

And now that I have climbed and won this height,
I must tread downward through the sloping shade
And travel the bewildering tracks till night.
                              —D. G. ROSSETTI

THE CRITICS of mountain books may complain with
some justice that they go on too long. The summit, or
as near to it as you may get, is the climax; everything
after it, bathos. But to the protagonists it is just that afterwards which is the real climax of the journey, for those
are the days of happiness 'pure and immaterial', the days
when the body is free to wander down the valleys or over
new, if smaller peaks; the spirit, untrammelled by
logistics, to absorb all that it had missed before. Over
these days a man likes to linger when he writes, oblivious
of the stern duty to finish dramatically. A postscript
chapter may be regarded as self-indulgence by the author;
and by the kindly reader, if it is not too long, as an easing
off in the story which is really part of its dènouement.

But duty, 'stern maid', hovers behind. I would have liked, for instance, to linger awhile in Charles's tunnel. On 1st June Charles had felt unwell, and had spent most of the day in bed. Tashi, a restless person of virtuous inclination, had suggested the tunnel and made a start by himself at the bergschrund. He found hard ice, and on the 2nd Charles joined in the work. While it was snowing they had kept warm and dry, and had even been able to watch for us in the afternoon, while Tashi gossiped of Sola Khumbu and past expeditions. The tunnel must have been fifteen feet long, and besides obviating the first, nasty jump off the ridge above, it allowed a safer stance for rope operations and for protecting us. (Plates 23*a* and *b*.)

I would have liked to dwell on the descent, but one or two vignettes only stick in mind. First the snow that fell all the night of the 3rd, and chased us down, fearful, towards the Nick next morning. As we were descending to Camp Two we stopped at Three, hardly able to see each other for the thick, determined flakes. It would be the last time, and we sorted out what would be needed below. There remained too much food, and in these unlikely surroundings we sat eating Family Assorted until we could eat no more. Down at Camp Two, in the late afternoon, the weather cleared in a way all the more wonderful for being so unusual, and for the previous murk. Slowly the curtains drew apart, the whole basin lay friendly under a westering sun. The snow dazzle made of each near jag a soft roundness that I wanted to stroke; each far summit looked at least twice its height. It was here, while Charles filmed tirelessly on the far side of our refuse crevasse, that my thoughts first turned seriously towards the peak we could see nobly situated in the very middle of the Sanctuary: Fluted Peak, as it was named, or more commonly Fluters. David's thoughts seemed to be moving in the same direction.

"What we really need is a cow mountain, after M.P.," we said.

* * *

I would have liked to dwell on the delights of Base, but to another they would be commonplace. The primulas were now going over, but many little potentillas peeped coyly from the crannies. Another peeper, not so coy, was the marten, who stole any food shamelessly and once carried off a closed butter pot, ate the contents and left lid and pot in different *caches*, along with half a dozen bars of chocolate, a meat bar, lemonade powder and other missing oddments. This time, as we lay discussing such diverse subjects as our finances, the probable arrival date of Moti and our children's education, there lurked no nagging thought that in a day or two we would be wrestling with one more improbability. Even the rain, when it came, could be mocked for coming too late. Physical pleasures are seldom keener, or more simple. The smell of scones cooking or the tingle of glacier water on skin were enough to send jaded senses into an ecstasy.

Charles was even moved by the *élan* to bathe; for the rest, the nip of a stand-up wash sufficed.

Voltaire maintained that man is unhappy because restless, and he would justly have accused the mountaineer of not staying long enough in the country through which he passes to notice it. Jimmy and Charles, as if to belie this traditional character, prepared to go down, slowly, through the Gurung villages. Jimmy, who had borne the burden of the expedition's arrangements, had also ends to tie up at Kathmandu, while Charles wanted to film Gurkha festivals. On 21st June we must be at Pokhara for the flight to Bhairwa, Lehra and the remote world.

This gave to David and myself, the restless reprobates, a week of holiday to play with, and Fluted Peak began to loom more distinctly as background to our plans. We reckoned its height 21,800 feet; its situation magnificent even though it is dominated from most angles by the giant rim which stretches from Annapurnas I to III. We would have the time for alternative routes. To reach the mountain would involve following Jimmy's 1956 line through the upper Modi gorge (See map, page 15). Then we would be in new country, we would enjoy the luxury of three Sherpas, since the needs of the others were modest, and besides all this, the weather looked better at last. (Vain delusion!) What more could a man ask of a week?

We left on 9th June, all but Tashi who waited for our delayed mail. Dikshya Man, joyful at his approaching release, wrung our hands once more in farewell. Later he confided to Charles that his burning desire to climb mountains had been converted into an equally burning desire to go hunting. Poor Dikshya Man. He had had a dull time. But we minded little as we climbed the moraine above camp and slithered down its dirty other side on to the still dirtier snout of the South Annapurna Glacier. This crossed, I built a cairn for the guidance of Tashi next day; it was immediately topped by a monster from the hand of Ang Tsering, for the cairn-building madness (and skill) is endemic among Sherpas. Soon the black cliffs of the upper Modi hemmed us in; our path lay up a grassy, scrambly shelf on its near bank, above the rough chocolate waters. At the first side-stream we turned up left, on to moraine. Ang Tsering's cairns became ever longer and more tapering. In the early afternoon, just short of the snout of West Glacier, an enormous rock overhang lured us to the left: the Cave, of which Jimmy had told us.

They must be bold spirits, the men of Chomrong. In the monsoon, with their flocks, they reach this cave across the lower slopes of Tent Peak, the nineteen-thousander which Jimmy had attempted. In the cave was wood, and no unwritten laws prevented the Sherpas from using it. There was peace here too, and beauty, when the cloud rolled back and Machapuchare floated above it, a dark triangle of rock, silver-edged.

A little way past the cave, the hillside above West Glacier flattened out in a broad shelf of grass up which, on the early morning of June 11th, the two of us wandered happily, on reconnaissance bent. Birds of every sort, from white-streaked snow pigeon to a delight-ful small blue bird, hopped and fluttered around. Soon our mountain appeared for a short time up on the left: a thing of airy, fluted ridges with a chaos of *séracs* some-where to the right, and to the right again the high col joining it to the rim. Sluggishly we climbed an enormous bulge of grass towards the long, low rock ridge which the mountain extended straight towards us. Having reached it, and found a camp site on pebbles among the snow, we descended in mist to the valley of the birds.

Tashi was wonderful, the pillar of our Sherpa society. But as I have said he held the firm belief that no camp site chosen by sahibs could be of any use at all. Next day he took one look at the proposed Camp One, and suggested moving right up under the ridge (its continuation visible in the left foreground, Plate 24*a*). At his site, therefore, and a very good one, we lay that afternoon re-reading letters, the news of home, children, friends, as strange and improbable and comforting as it always is in a snow-bound tent. Our undamped optimism put the height at 17,000 feet; probably it was no more than 16,000. When the afternoon drizzle stopped, David and I reconnoitred on up the trough between rock ridge and fantasia of *séracs* on West Glacier. It was the only possible route; but in the mist we could see nothing except that, with interruptions, the trough continued for some way.

There might be something unæsthetic about the after-noon dullness, but to make up for it there was a bright-ness, a luminous blue radiance in the air of morning.

Packing up was no hardship with three Sherpas vying in attentions. At 4.40 on the 12th Tashi could be heard coughing over the Primus, Ang Tsering, as was his wont, chanting the sacred words. At 6.30, with one tent and two Sherpas, we were away. In one place a crevasse from West Glacier, biting its way right over to the rock wall, gave an awkward step. But in an hour we were well past our reconnaissance point and on a wide plain rimmed with shining peaks. To the north the turbulent West Glacier lapped up against the great unnamed wall whose fragments tumble constantly to feed it. What we called Glacier Dome (23,800 feet) shone straight ahead like a huge bald monk's crown against the blue. And there, beyond the silvery saddle to which its left-hand skyline dropped, our peak stood up boldly once more, refusing to be dominated. Its obvious but sharp south ridge we ruled out, with memories of Machapuchare. The only other course, and it did not look so easy now, was to continue up our glacier trough, round the right-hand skyline ridge, and then either continue to the col, or climb the north-east face behind, invisible but for an enormous finger of a *sérac*, perhaps 200 feet high.

The trough surprised us with an awkward ice-rock chimney or two—taken light-heartedly by the Sherpas—but it did lead round the base of the ridge, and by the time the mist descended we were on another plateau, very convenient for camping. The sahibs stopped. Tashi, however, looked at this site as if it were one worse even than the last, and pointed upwards at all that we

Fluted Peak : the route goes round the corner to the right, then back

Fluted Peak : on the summit block, the first attempt

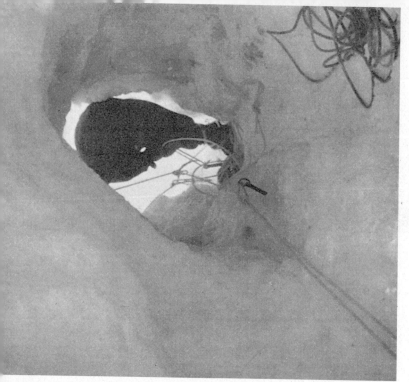

Inside the tunnel

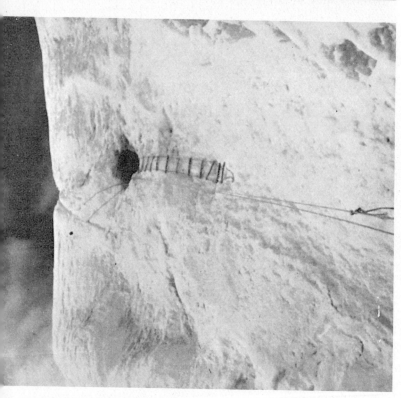

Near the top of the cut-off: Wylie's tunnel

could see of the mountain: the bottoms of two gullies disappearing into mist 400 feet above our heads. Two hundred feet below these the slope jutted out unexpectedly, like a springboard, overhung below. Towards this ledge, obedient but cursing the heat, the snow and Tashi, we toiled slowly on and had to admit that it again was a very nice site. Tent up, tea made, dejection gone and a happy conversation with Tashi, which seemed to be about a prospective visit to England. Then the Sherpas tramped cautiously off, promising to return tomorrow and take down the tent. What luxury, to have camp carried, pitched and fetched! And what idleness of the mountaineer who chooses to climb in Nepal, rather than carry his own baggage in stern Chitral!

For the last time I fretted and worried at the snow falling in the afternoon. It will be the last time, I kept saying, tomorrow it won't matter. But it did matter today, the patter-patter, the pauses, the anxious peeps outside into brown blankets over everything. At supper-time it was still snowing, lightly but as if it would go on for ever. Towards 8 o'clock in the evening it stopped.

We had overestimated our height as usual: 19,000 against a probable 18,000 feet. Let's start earlier still, we said, by moonlight in the Alpine tradition. Again a restless night, this time porridge cooked the night before to heat, this time a torch, and at 3.15 a.m. we stepped into a blinding silver light. The peaks, sheeted in new snow, lay sleeping under an almost full moon. Only where we stood the shadow still fell dark from the great face above.

We must be up that gully and down before the sun loosens things, we said, and started towards the right-hand of the two. Steep snow, hard with little ice patches, lay packed between grim rock buttresses. We took the kicking and chipping in turns and made height fast, losing the sense of time. The gully gave out below a bigger face, in the grey half-light a huge thing of mighty *séracs*. A vertical wall, apparently some 400 feet high, barred our way. There was only one line: a second gully, just to its left, in the centre of the face. We took that, with some misgivings as to what we might have to share it with, and passed the 200-foot *sérac* which was really a break-away from the vertical wall.

A little ice near the top; but the blood was up now, and we had espied a broad shelf leading out right, above the vertical wall. It was an escape line, the only reasonable way. Having plodded some distance along it we stopped, tired by over three hours' effort and satisfied that the top was near.

We were wrong, of course. Even as we sat munching chocolate it was clear that more of the mountain remained above. A tramp to the right revealed a whole tier of it, gently fluted. The sun was now hot on our shoulder, the early mystery gone. In an access of desperation we took the new obstacle fast, changing lead frequently. Above it, surely, must be the summit ridge. At about 8 a.m.—but I never dared look at the time—we were stepping out on to the upper east ridge, at this point a broad hummocky highway. One moment we stopped for another look at Machapuchare, blue and distinct and graceful, holding her long north ridge out like an arm towards her taller brothers, haloed in blue. Then we turned west.

The summit was there, quite obvious, some 200 yards up the ridge. What was not so obvious was how to reach it. It looked as if the playful giant had taken a large block of ice, over a hundred feet each way, and dumped it gently on the very top. Sun and frost had furrowed it a little, allowing a snow mantle to settle; the crown had been cushioned with snow. But the sides remained steep, and the frontal ridge looked excessive. I suggested trying round to the left. This took me, with step-cutting, over a steep shoulder, and David came up to belay me. The top could only be fifty feet above, just over the eave. To the right a traverse of a few feet—but on almost vertical ice, and we had no pitons. As this was to be the cow mountain after M.P., we had never thought to bring them. To the left lay a traverse faintly less steep, but masked with softening snow. I dug out a few steps (Plate 24b) then retreated in a quiver, uncertain of any footing at all. "Oh the little further, and how much it seems!" We went down, having lost a good hour, and started on the frontal line after all.

We should have known by now that things seen end-on are not as bad as they look. All the same, twenty feet near the top were as steep as anything on the expedition: a hard little facet where the ridge abutted, hard enough to take cut handholds when the angle threw me right out of balance. A few steps, and I could get a left leg far out on the snowy crest. A shift of balance, carefully so as not to disturb the handhold, a body poised in a tableau of silver and blue—and we were up.

The highest point lay some yards along the cushion. We spent only fifteen minutes there, and these tinged with anxiety since the time was 9.30 on a hot morning, much too late. I took a round of photographs, balancing the leveller on my knee while I swallowed sardines at the same time. David noted the angles. But I shall never forget the scene, for it impressed itself on that subconscious, untroubled memory which has the power to push its images to the surface in later days. The whole Sanctuary lay revealed, and round it every peak: Hiunchuli and Ganesh, and the long ridge to Annapurna I, whose south-east face seemed almost to be hanging above us. Then along over the Glacier Dome to Gangapurna and the great bulk of Annapurna III, and beyond that the flattened rise of IV, sharply topped by the neat cone of II. In front of these the bristling, broken ridge that led southward, to the fairy delicacy of Machapuchare queening it for all her slighter stature over every giant around. She was incomparable. Postscript chapters may be frowned upon; but for me this was the true climax of the expedition: a summit, and the sight of that supreme pyramid, the goddess-haunted, under whose very crest we suppliants had been allowed to stand.

At the time, however, it seemed far from a climax. Those plump cloudlets that played round Machapuchare's base would mean snow, in an hour or two, for our high hopes of the weather had changed into stoical expectation of the worst. We must get down soon. On the frontal passage we managed a knight's move, awkward but not so awkward as direct descent. Then, as fast as possible, we made off down the broad highway, down the tier of now rotten flutings—and the snow started. Between here and the top of the higher gully we blessed our one or two marker flags. Down the gully we kicked, as fast as we safely could, seeing very little but the foot or two around, kicking hard to find the firm ground, looking over shoulders for the next marker flag. Near the top of the lower gully we came upon a passage which had worried us on the way up, an incipient shoulder on which powder snow had drifted almost knee-deep. Just here David shouted: "Look out!" and along the line of his steps, just beside me, a whole top layer of snow, without warning, went slithering with a gentle hiss into the speckled gloom below.

It was a thoughtful moment; but after initial dismay we agreed that this might also be a blessing, since anything now left in the gullies would be firm. In the event it proved almost too firm, for our toes wore themselves out kicking into a hardened substratum of old snow. Moreover in the lower jaws, as we at last entered them, little patches of ice had been left on a rock bed: a nasty final problem. However, by that time we could hear the shouts of Tashi and Da Temba, not far below. At 1.15 p.m. we were on the little shelf, drinking un-

135

savoury but delectable tea while they packed the tent.

It was a wet journey down, but it was the last. By 4 p.m., back at Camp One, we were lying with sore toes and grateful hearts drinking more tea. There was not much to eat, but it did not matter. In five days out we had climbed our mountain, 'at the first go'. Outside the snow drummed on, and the sound was music to my ears.

CHAPTER TEN

Envoi

*If I were asked the most agreeable thing in life, I
should say it is the pleasure of contrast. One cannot
imagine anyone but an angel sitting with a harp in
Paradise for ever. The ordinary human being needs
a change.*

—FREYA STARK

THERE IS PLEASURE in contrast, and it is this pleasure
which I have found at its keenest in the Himalaya. In the
Antarctic, I imagine, it comes too suddenly after months
and even years of the monotony of snow. In Nepal you
may get it three or four times during one expedition, and
the last time the most deliciously of all. That is why,
though we were short of some foods and sensual enough
to miss them, though leeches beset us in the gorge and
though we were several times pelted with rain while the
familiar thunder rolled around, the walk back through
the valleys fittingly closed our experience. Charles and
Jimmy, I think, found the same in their visits to the
villages that line the path.

I remember reflecting, as David and I rested at Hinko with the coolies who had come up for our kit, that imaginative literature must be impossible up here. In that sense of relaxed, rather selfish well-being that comes after effort, I marvelled that I had only a year ago written a novel, and decided then and there that it had been an impossible task. What person accustomed to action has ever been able to write of characters he has not seen, experiences he has not had himself? Cook or Park, Stanley or Sven Hedin, Scott or Shackleton, Tilman or Shipton? Their own experiences, yes, splendidly told, but that seemed to me a much easier task. The sea fares best, perhaps, with Melville and Conrad, and the air with Saint-Exupéry. But it seemed to me also, as I looked back, that all that had happened in the last months had been so personal, so bound up with living friends, with Charles and David, with Jimmy and Roger, with the Sherpas, that the experience could never distil itself away from their known faces, any more than the mountain could forgo that great shape which had dominated our waking thoughts. If I should write now, it must be of what I had seen.

The real farewell came on our last day's walk to Pokhara, as we descended the broad ridge above Naudanra. To the right, looking down, we could see the Phewa Tal glistening far beyond the tiers of thatched huts—for all the world like Derwentwater from Skiddaw. To look forward to there was the reunion with Charles and tea at the Mission (this was to take place in another storm, faced with as much *insouciance* as the first); there was Lehra and a bath, good food and Jimmy's smile, the knowledge that our affairs were in his capable hands; there was Delhi and the aeroplane, and the joyful reunion with families at the end of the journey. There was much to look forward to.

But behind us stood the mountain, a great stark monolith above the trees, snow-powdered by the storms and twin-topped, breaking through the horizontal snows of the other peaks. For the last time we tried desperately to capture it with clicking cameras. To me it represented, in those moments, something simple and big, on which thought could focus placidly. It represented slopes and pitons and tents, Sherpas and Gurungs and *jharal*, all those things and people that had occupied us. These could be complicated in detail at times, as we knew, but directed to an end so simply black and white that it made mock of the confusing infinity of greys that compose life's other operations. Ours had become a dream world, almost, now to disappear, and there must be sorrow at the disappearance, at the good-bye. Even as I looked back at the mountain the morning clouds, now early afloat, were rising, slowly but ruthlessly, to swallow it. The scarf which had been thrown negligently round its shoulders swelled to hide its head. Soon our own experience would vanish, even as this queen of peaks was vanishing before my eyes.

Ecstasy, I thought, is found in the brief resting time between the effort of the exploring body and the sterner mental effort that awaits—the doubts and decisions, even the delights of return. Then we must be doing again, assuming responsibility; but not now. And yet we pass through this happiness, as we pass through most of the good moments in life, so quickly that they are gone almost before we notice them. That is why, transposing time and place, I wanted to cry out, on that green turf above Naudanra: "If there be a Paradise on earth, it is now, it is now, it is now!" And the sage whose words I echoed would forgive me for acknowledging that Paradise is no less real for being limited, in time as well as place.

Two more *jeux d'esprit*

FOR WHICH MACHAPUCHARE

IS RESPONSIBLE

1. *Trams and Trains*

Away, good God! with trams and trains
and standing in the endless queue
and catching buses when it rains
and work, and chores I *have* to do.
Away with my employer's eye
and office tea, unmixed with love,
and typing trash, and wondering why,
and clocks with hands that will not move.
Away with prams, say I, that we
must push because the neighbours do
by railed-in park and cemetery,
on paths so neat, past flowers so few.
Let me not eat from tins, great God,
but feed upon an air that's clean;
up valleys that no foot has trod
see snows till now by man unseen.

Let me go climb those virgin snows,
leave the dark stain of man behind.
Let me adventure—and heaven knows
grateful shall be my quiet mind.

Now I'm alone, and I'm afraid.
The wind is cold, the stars are high.
Coffee and cake were surely made
to ease a mountain's cruelty.
The ice peak is before me still,
a ghost white-masked, a monster form;
weakly my heart bends to my will,
my chilled hands cringe in the glove to warm.
Mist creeps from the valley floor
and camp's a hundred miles away.
A flake falls, two snowflakes more,
the air is dyed to dunnest grey.
My comrade's turned, and I'm alone.
Great God! for all the homely things,
for Primrose Villa, for the one
answer to foolish questionings!
For gas, for baths, for buttered toast,
for cosy buses when it rains,
for Lyons' lunch, for work the most—
Praise be to God for trams and trains!

2. *The Snowslide*

It came so slow.
I remember, we sweated and cursed across the bulge
of the white snow sloping; our tongues dry and our shirts
clung on our legs; loads bit at our back
till we sat down.
Then, from above, the murmur of little men,
rustle and click and roll of a loosened line
as they came flickering, flocking out from the jaws
where the gully held them, gently curious down.
Just a line of snowballs, as on a Christmas lawn
a child quarries and rolls, and rolling along
they are bigger and bigger; but lawns do not tilt and turn
over, then down.
You were below, when the loping invaders came,
pawed at my arm, but the ice-axe held and they passed
disappointed to you, rock in the swell of seas,
too tough for this wash ever to break your hold,
it came so slow.
But they came and came, and their gathering overbore
gently and slow, gently they carried you down
like a king reclining—look! where the crisping snow
rolled into nothing, eyes to the green beyond.
Then there was silence, hiss of the slide soft hushed.
The mountains lay, stood, reared like creatures that dream
lovely in sunlight: ebony, silver and silk
just as before. But I loathed them, trembling and sick,
for you had gone.

Two Notes by James Roberts

1. *Permission and Customs*

Permission for an expedition to enter Nepal is obtained through the Foreign Office, which in turn refers the request to the British Embassy at Kathmandu.

Before forwarding the request to the Ministry of Foreign Affairs of the Government of Nepal, the British Embassy normally requires proof of the experience and integrity of the party, since in recommending an application to the Ministry of Foreign Affairs the Ambassador is to some extent accepting responsibility for the good behaviour of the party while it is in Nepal.

An expedition sponsored by the Everest Foundation will normally be accepted by the British Embassy. But in 1956 the recommendation of the Royal Geographical Society alone was not sufficient.

Regulations imposed by the Nepalese Government on expeditions include the payment of an expedition royalty, employment of a liaison officer, a scale of compensation for death or injuries suffered by the liaison officer, Sherpas or porters, and certain restrictions on news, copyright and the use of photographs.

The scale of royalty is adjusted according to the height of the peak. In 1956 the Government was much concerned with 'named' peaks and heights above sea level. This may restrict the freedom of a small mobile party; but it should be possible to reach a compromise, so long as the area of exploration is properly defined to the Government and an undertaking given not to climb peaks of above, say, 22,000 feet.

In giving permission for an expedition the Government will normally also grant 'Customs facilities'. This should be got in writing—if only in a letter from the British Embassy—for use on the border.

India in turn, approached through the Office of the U.K. High Commission in New Delhi, will allow expedition goods to be taken in bond from the port of entry to the Nepalese border, where the seals are examined and a signature must be obtained. There are various official forms, supplied by the U.K. High Commission, to be filled in.

Goods declared for consumption in Nepal are not charged on by the Indian Government, but a sum of money must be deposited with a bank—or a guarantee must be signed—to cover the Customs value of goods to be re-exported out of Nepal, and then out of India, at the end of the expedition. Once the goods have been exported, the guarantee is cancelled. Thus on winding up an expedition the party must be at pains to obtain the following evidence:

(a) Certified list (by Ministry of Foreign Affairs) of goods expended in Nepal.

(b) List of goods re-exported. This second list must be checked and signed at the border, and bonded; then sent to the agents at the original port of entry, who must satisfy the Indian Customs that the goods leave the country.

2. *The Spelling of Machapuchare*

The spelling on the Survey map is Machhapuchhare. Wilfrid Noyce wrote asking me to reduce the number of aitches, implying that I was half responsible for the mountain anyway. During the expedition we spelt it like that, sometimes in two words, sometimes in one. It was a good word to roll round one's tongue.

The translation is of course Fishtail (or Fish's Tail). On receiving this *cri de cœur* (he said that in England Machhapuchhare could never be taken seriously) I took out my own Nepali dictionary (Kilgour 1923) and looked up 'Fish'. I found '*Machchha*'—one more aitch than before. I closed the volume hurriedly and searched out Sir Ralph Turner's standard work. Here I was relieved to find it became '*Macha*'. In some excitement I now turned to 'Tail', and found '*Puchar*' or '*Pucchar* . Aitches I can take, but not more c's. So let it be 'Machapuchare', the first two a's long, the last very short.

The expedition is indebted to the following for gifts:

Airmed Ltd.—oxygen masks.
B.B.C. Television—cine film.
Bird, Alfred and Sons, Ltd.—Grape-Nuts.
Bowater-Eburite Sales Ltd.—fiberite packing cases.
British Drug Houses—medical equipment.
Brown and Polson Ltd.—glucose tablets.
Chivers Ltd.—jams and dehydrated potato.
Costa, G., and Co.—Knorr Soups.
Huntley and Palmers Ltd.—biscuits.
Imperial Tobacco Co., Ltd.—cigarettes and tobacco.
Kraft Foods Ltd.—cheese.
Mars Ltd.—sweets.
Moll and Baucher Ltd.—Antarctic cloth.
Nestlé Co., Ltd.—dried milk, Nescafé.
Normalair Ltd. (A. W. Bridge)—loan of oxygen cylinders.
Peek Frean and Co., Ltd.—biscuits.
Pindisports Ltd.—tent and equipment, Sherpas' clothing, etc.
Quaker Oats Ltd.—porridge.
Rowntrees Ltd.—chocolate.
Ryvita Co., Ltd.—Ryvita.
Sifta Salt Ltd.—Salties.

Sports Illustrated—colour film.
Tate and Lyle Ltd.—sugar.
Three Cooks Ltd.—powder drinks and soup.
Welch and Sons, Ltd.—sweets.
Whiteside, H. S., and Co., Ltd.—nuts.
Wiper, Robert—Kendal Mint Cake.

We thank the following for food and equipment at cost price or at reduced prices:

Bell and Howell Ltd.—cine accessories.
British Ropes Ltd.—nylon line.
British Visqueen Ltd.—polythene bags, etc.
Condrup Ltd.—Primus spares, etc.
Edgington, Benjamin, Ltd.—equipment.
Flint, Howard, Ltd.—windproof clothing.
Haynes and Cann Ltd.—high-altitude boots.
Ilford Ltd.—film.
Kenyon, Wm., Ltd.—manila rope.
Lawrie, Robert, Ltd.—climbing equipment.
Leitz, Ernst (Instruments), Ltd.—photographic equipment.
Ministry of Food—meat bars, dehydrated vegetables.
Prestige Group Ltd.—Prestige cookers.
Rowntrees Ltd.—chocolate.
War Office—mountaineering equipment.

Finally we must thank *Benjamin Edgington Ltd.*, who did the packing.

A Very Few Technical Terms

The public is so well educated in mountaineering termi-
nology these days that a glossary hardly seems necessary.
There are, however, one or two terms which may puzzle
some, while the use of one or two special items of equipment may interest others. I have cut these to a minimum.

belay—a safeguard with the rope. On rock this is usually
a projection round which it can be put; on ice we
used pitons driven in, to which rope slings could be
attached. On snow the axe is driven in, if possible to
the head, and the rope wound round it.

bergschrund (or just *schrund*)—a crevasse or chasm formed
where a steep slope meets a flattish glacier surface.

chimney—ice chimneys were a feature of the final face. A
vertical furrow in the ice surface some three or four
feet wide, into which a man can get.

couloir—beyond a certain width a chimney becomes a
couloir or gully which may be a number of yards
wide.

crevasse—a fissure in a glacier, often of great depth.

fluting—vertical ribbing and furrowing in a snow face. It

is a feature of mountains in the Himalaya, usually between 21,000 and 23,000 feet.

gendarme—a tower on a ridge.

karabiner (or *snap-ring*)—a metal, spring-loaded clip which can be fixed to rope or piton.

névé—a snowfield, usually flat.

piton (or *peg*)—a metal spike (some of ours were cylindrical, some U-shaped) with a ring at its head. This is driven into the ice and used in conjunction with a karabiner to secure the rope passing between two climbers, or to take a fixed rope.

roping down (or *abseil* or *rappel*)—a method of descent by doubling the rope and putting it round a projection or sling, then lowering oneself.

sérac—a tower or pinnacle of ice.

traverse—horizontal or diagonal crossing of a mountain slope.